Siegfried Bernfeld (1892-1?) regarded member of Sigmu... circle, who in 1927 settled in San Francisco, where he continued his career as a distinguished analyst and teacher. Freud called him "an outstanding expert of psychoanalysis, the strongest head among my students and followers, an extremely powerful teacher."

In this book, originally published in 1925, Bernfeld projects the outline of a future science of education. His conception of science, however, has little in common with behaviorist conditioning as currently exemplified by Burrhus F. Skinner. It is much broader and does not eliminate individual responsibility for human growth. Bernfeld urges the members of the educational profession to learn the psychic and social realities of their work, or see their labors condemned to the futility of Sisyphus. He is especially critical of the limitless and narcissistic idealism of the so-called great educators who built their theories around noble ends without coming to terms with the means of their realization.

Bernfeld's account of psychic reality is derived from Freud, and reminds the educator that an inescapable element of all education is the inhibition of instinctual drives and their redirection toward cultural goals. Such redirection generates crises and frustrations that must be accepted as a necessary part of human growth.

The social realities Bernfeld views in the perspective of Marx: ideologies that employ education in the exploitative interests of mi- views with skepticism and never forgets how precarious an enterprise human education must always remain.

The translator, Frederic Lilge, is Professor of Education at the University of California, Berkeley, and has written on German and Soviet education. Peter Paret, author of the Preface, is Professor of European History at Stanford University.

Sisyphus, or *the Limits of Education*

SIEGFRIED BERNFELD

Sisyphus *or*
The Limits of Education

Translated by Frederic Lilge

Foreword by Anna Freud
Preface by Peter Paret

UNIVERSITY OF CALIFORNIA PRESS
BERKELEY, LOS ANGELES, LONDON

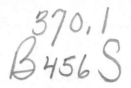

Original German title:
Sisyphos oder die Grenzen der Erziehung

Published by Suhrkamp Verlag, Frankfurt am Main, 1967.
Originally published by Internationaler Psychoanalytischer
Verlag, Leipzig, Wien, Zürich, 1925.

University of California Press
Berkeley and Los Angeles, California
University of California Press, Ltd.
London, England
Copyright © 1973, by
The Regents of the University of California
ISBN: 0-520-01407-3
Library of Congress Catalog Card Number: 77-84784
Printed in the United States of America
Designed by Jean Peters

Contents

Foreword

In the book before us, first published in 1925, Siegfried Bernfeld discusses problems of education which have not changed much during the intervening years. The educational theoreticians with their ideals and hopes are as far removed from practical reality as they were half a century ago. Education itself is as limited as it was then by the given personalities of the adults in charge of children, by the personalities of the children themselves and by the social environment within which their growing up takes place. Also, what the author calls the "constants" of education are still with us, i.e. the adults' loving and aggressive attitudes towards children. Parents and educators search as before for the balance between praise and punishment, permissiveness and frustration which is most likely to promote growth. It hardly needs mention that also another of the author's contentions remains valid: that the educational systems as such, far from being revolutionary, are always conservative, in so far as they represent a society's attempts to transmit its values to the next generation.

Nevertheless there are changes since Siegfried Bernfeld's time in the spread of knowledge concerning child development. The psychoanalytic tenets of child psychology which he quotes tentatively and carefully as the new information on which better education might be based, have grown and increased and represent now a formidable body of knowledge. Guided by them, we come closer to realising the possibilities and impossibilities of changing the instinctual nature of the child and of assessing the benefits as well as the possible damage done to it by educational interference. These are advances to be welcomed. They will be all the more beneficial if we approach them and make use of them in the same spirit of criticism and scepticism which pervades the present book and gives it its especial value.

Anna Freud

Anna Freud is director of the Hampstead Child-Therapy Course and Clinic in London.

Preface: SISYPHUS AND ITS AUTHOR

When *Sisyphus* was published in 1925, Siegfried Bernfeld, still in his early thirties, had already written half a dozen books on such seemingly diverse subjects as the psychology of infants and adolescents, Zionism, education, and psychoanalytic theory and method. This variety did not reflect a fragmentation of thought; as Bernfeld treated it, each theme bore on the others, and all were marked by an acute sense of social responsibility that had found in psychoanalysis a prerequisite for changing society: the means of understanding human nature. The books and the many articles that accompanied them were not solely the products of speculation but also of varied and intensely felt practical experience. Since his student days before 1914, Bernfeld had been an organizer of youth movements, editor, academic psychologist, soldier, functionary in Jewish organizations, commandant of the Jewish self-defense force in Vienna during the 1918 revolution, founder of an experimental school, practicing analyst, and a teacher of psychoanalysis. To some degree, *Sisyphus* bears the imprint of all these activities. It is a compressed statement of ideas that its author had developed and applied since his adolescence —and a highly combative statement at that. A reviewer of the first edition called the book "a blast on the last trumpet for authoritarian teachers and also for that new breed of educators proclaiming the gospel of love." That was too optimistic; but *Sisyphus* did have a permanently liberating influence on many of its readers, and the book retains its significance as a document of the times and as one of the more provocative diagnoses of the ills and possibilities of pedagogy in the history of education. Its historical character, like that of all successful intellectual efforts, is combined with a strong relevance to the present.

Bernfeld was born in 1892, the son of a Jewish wholesale merchant established in Vienna.[1] After acquiring a sound Gymnasium education, he entered the University of Vienna, where he studied biology, social and educational psychology, and mathematics. When he was twenty-one he published his first psychoanalytically oriented paper, "On the Unconscious Determination of the Thought-Process: A Self-Observation," and began to experiment with self-analysis and the analysis of dreams and symptoms of fellow students. Although himself exceptionally successful in his academic work, he came to believe that too frequently educational institutions distorted the processes of learning and of growing up by exaggerating the student's need to prepare for adult life rather than helping him cope with the trials of adolescence and post-adolescence. As a first step toward improvement he founded, in 1912, the Academic Committee for School Reform, which soon attracted several thou-

[1] I am here discussing only those aspects of Bernfeld's life that have a bearing on the ideas and the writing of *Sisyphus*. Two comprehensive biographical accounts are his obituary by Hedwig Hoffer in *The International Journal of Psycho-Analysis*, xxxvi, no. 1 (Jan.-Feb. 1955), pp. 66–71; and Rudolf Eckstein's "Siegfried Bernfeld, 1892–1953," in *Psychoanalytic Pioneers*, ed. Franz Alexander, Samuel Eisenstein, and Marin Grotjahn, New York–London, 1966.

sand members from German and Austrian universities and secondary schools.[2] The A. C. S. was inspired by the views of Gustav Wyneken, the prophet of progressive education in Germany, who regarded students as the pioneers of a spiritual and cultural regeneration, a renewal that Wyneken, in this respect representative of most of the German youth movement before 1914, saw in apolitical terms. Bernfeld tried to underpin Wyneken's rather mystic, bourgeois ideal of a new youth culture with the beginnings of a coherent psychology of puberty, and added to it a socialistic program of education that called for the destruction of middleclass domination of the schools. In schools and universities A. C. S. chapters spread their message of the equality of the sexes, the injustice of class differences, the need to emancipate youth from the values of the adult world. A journal with the hopeful title *Der Anfang* printed contributions by A. C. S. members, which, Wyneken and Bernfeld expected, would contain reliable information about the feelings and needs of young people and lead to a common program of action. Among its regular authors was the young Walter Benjamin, who only recently, decades after his death, has been recognized as one of Germany's most interesting critics and essayists between the wars. For some time he and Bernfeld worked together, though Benjamin, then still holding high hopes for the spiritual enlightenment of his generation, shared neither Bernfeld's political activism nor

[2] The history of the A. C. S. can be followed in the pages of its journal *Der Anfang*, of which Bernfeld was co-editor, and in Bernfeld's book *Die Schulgemeinde und ihre Funktion im Klassenkampf*, Berlin, 1928. A good summary, which however contains several errors about Bernfeld's later life and work, is given by Heinrich Kupffer in *Gustav Wyneken*, Stuttgart, 1970, pp. 74–80. Walter Z. Laqueur has analyzed the social and ideological conditions in which the A. C. S. existed in his study *Young Germany: A History of the German Youth Movement*, London, 1962.

his interest in developing a scientific basis for the uniqueness of *Jugendkultur*.[3]

The insight that guided Bernfeld's psychological research, he defined in the first issue of *Der Anfang*: "Childhood and youth are not purposeless, transitional stages on the way to maturity, but essential steps in human development, complete within themselves. Youth and maturity do not differ in degree, but are qualitatively different. Consequently youth is not incomplete and unripe maturity, but a complete condition in itself."[4] Psychologists, teachers, and society as a whole, by recognizing the particular needs of the young, could help them become happier—the best preparation for adult life. The institutional implication was also clear: adults should be slow to impose their concerns and methods on the young. For example, students freed from oppressive discipline and sharing in the administration of their schools would learn more willingly and to better effect. At the same time, their healthy psychological growth depended on adult guidance and on some denials and restrictions—*Sisyphus* contains some references to these—and even reformed institutions might need protection against the young, an early recognition whose accuracy Bernfeld found confirmed by his subsequent experiences as a teacher and therapist, and by such spectacles of the twenties and thirties as the disruption by sincere, idealistic German students of the lectures of academics whose views they conceived to be immoral.

In 1914, after some preliminary legal harrassment, the police dissolved the A. C. S.; the war would in any case

[3] Kupffer, *op. cit.*, p. 79.
[4] Fourteen years later, in his pamphlet *Die heutige Psychologie der Pubertät*, Leipzig-Vienna-Zürich, 1927, p. 14, Bernfeld repeated this statement in the course of a vigorous attack on the claim by the philosopher Eduard Spranger that youth wants and needs to be led.

soon have put a stop to it. It remains an interesting episode in the history of the German youth movement, which with the exception of its Socialist and to some extent its Catholic groups was headed in quite a different direction, and for a young man to have organized it almost singlehanded was a remarkable achievement. His exceptional empathy with children and students that made Bernfeld's success with the A. C. S. possible never left him; and even in those early days he was an unusually persuasive teacher. Among the many instances of these qualities that I myself witnessed in him, one in particular stands out. I relate it here since it is in any case time to declare my personal interest in the author of *Sisyphus*.

In 1932 my mother moved to Vienna to study with Sigmund Freud, and two years later married Bernfeld. My small sister and especially I, children of an earlier marriage, naturally encountered our new stepfather with suspicion, to which he responded with unobtrusive understanding and affection. Since Viennese primary schools had little to recommend them at that time it was decided that I should be educated by a tutor, to which the school authorities were agreeable, provided I passed a qualifying examination. My stepfather prepared me for this ordeal, not least by telling me that the examination was absurd but worth passing since the schools would then leave me in peace; all went better than expected, even when the civics teacher demanded the names, from West to East, of the twenty-odd bridges that cross the Danube in the Vienna district. When I returned home I found a present from my stepfather—an aquarium with tropical fish—in celebration of the event. I asked how he could have bought the aquarium before he knew that I had passed; to which he answered that passing was important, but that I had to take the examination was more important, and he *had* know that. As is true of every good teacher, he was more concerned with internal development than with external success.

Bernfeld's service in the first World War was spent in Vienna, apart from a rather Schweikian interlude when he accompanied a military mission to Turkey as a non-Turkish-speaking interpreter. He welcomed the approaching dissolution of the monarchy, which he hoped would be replaced by political and social conditions more favorable to the working classes and the Jews. Refugees from the Russian front impressed him with the urgency and complexity of the Jewish question in Central and Eastern Europe.[5] Already in 1916, in an article in Martin Buber's journal *Der Jude,* he argued that the influx of displaced Jewish children that might be expected as a result of Austrian defeats in Galicia would present severe problems of welfare and education, but also great opportunities. Should these children receive haphazard instruction in the traditional religious schools and orphanages of the Jewish community, to return after the war to their native ghettoes or to join the Jewish proletariat of the European and American cities? Or was this an occasion for an educational and political experiment in a new kind of school that might restore the traumatized children to health and train them to be self-reliant farmers, workers, and craftsmen in Palestine

[5] This phase of Bernfeld's work is discussed by Willi Hoffer in his admirable article "Siegfried Bernfeld and 'Jerubbaal'," in the *Year Book of the Leo Baeck Institute,* x (1965). Hoffer met Bernfeld in 1919 and they soon became close friends, collaborating in the experimental school Bernfeld founded as well as in several publications dealing with the psychology and creativity of youth. In the 1930's Hoffer settled in London, and later became president of the British Psycho-Analytical Society and editor of *The International Journal of Psycho-Analysis.* I am grateful for the kindness with which before his death in 1967 he responded to my questions about the early history of psychoanalytically oriented education.

or in the autonomous Jewish districts that some people thought would be established in eastern Europe?[6] Bernfeld's appeal evoked no concrete response at the time, though his prediction of a vast human tragedy was only too accurate. Three years later he himself, on a small scale, tried to put his ideas into practice.

In March 1918 Bernfeld founded a new journal, *Jerubbaal*, that sought to reconcile the opposing Zionist and Socialist factions within Austrian Jewry and create a youth movement as an advance guard of the Jewish nationalism that he hoped was emerging. The journal's name, his friend Willi Hoffer writes, was taken from the episode in the Book of Judges in which Gideon and ten other youths "faced up to and acted against the hypocrisy, falsehood, and opportunism of their elders who worshipped both Jahve and Baal. It was a revolt in which the elders . . . [were] given time for learning from the young and for admitting their failure, a victory of the young over the old, but not amounting to parricide, free from guilt, true heroism." But, Hoffer continues, "it was a dangerous emblem which Bernfeld and those who supported him had chosen; one need hardly enlarge on it. The symbol expressed, and Bernfeld must have known it, of course, the idea that youth contains a revolutionary, even destructive element which if unleashed and not controlled by knowledge and experience, not to speak of wisdom, can as well destroy as it can create and build."[7] In the spring of 1918 the time had not yet come for action, whether destructive or constructive; the first requirement was to mobilize the Jewish minority into a politically effective pressure group. Again Bernfeld resorted to the lever of the young. In May he organized and

[6] "Die Kriegswaisen," *Der Jude*, i (1916), pp. 269–271.
[7] W. Hoffer, *op. cit.*, p. 156.

presided over a three-day rally of Jewish youths, which ended with the founding of the "Association of the Jewish Youth of Austria" with Bernfeld as president. To provide intellectual and vocational instruction without which a nationalist Jewish mass movement could never coalesce, he established a progressive training college for teachers—the *Paedagogium*. The relationship between these activist bodies and the regular Jewish organizations was not smooth; but by the summer of 1918 the breakup of the monarchy was at hand, and the political situation now demanded the cooperation of all factions. Like other ethnic groups, the Austrian Jews formed a comprehensive association to defend their interests, and Bernfeld became a member of the secretariat of the Vienna district. When the Jewish National Council was founded early in November, he was placed in charge of its section on education and vocational counseling.[8]

It indicates the pitiful political weakness of Austrian Jewry and helps us understand the urgency of Bernfeld's Zionist activities that the overriding concern of the Viennese Jews when the revolution broke out was to protect themselves against physical attack. Especially alarming were the large numbers of Polish soldiers, many still armed, who were passing through the capital on their way home, and the daily reports of looting and violence in the streets gained additional gravity from the first rumors of pogroms

[8] To some extent the activities of Bernfeld and of the groups with which he was associated can be traced in the weekly *Jüdische Zeitung*. It was however something of an establishment voice and tended to minimize the more radical groups as well as many of the extralegal or informal actions that occurred during the revolution. For the following I am indebted to two of Bernfeld's associates at the time, whom I interviewed in London in July 1972: Dr. Robert Weltsch, of the Leo Baeck Institute in London, and Dr. Scholem Adler-Rudel, now of Tel Aviv.

in Galicia. As the Jewish organizations were slow to act, Bernfeld took the initiative and formed a few hundred demobilized Jewish servicemen into a self-defense force. The Jewish Youth Hostel became the headquarters of this body, whose members wore armbands with the blue and white Zionist colors, and were equipped with rifles, pistols, and even a few machine guns that Bernfeld appropriated from an army storehouse. In a talk with Karl Seitz, since Victor Adler's death head of the Austrian Socialists and president of the Council of State, Bernfeld informed him of the existence of his force, which would protect the Jewish quarter until the new government had established its authority—an offer that Seitz, according to Bernfeld's recollection, accepted with relief. For some days, Jewish soldiers policed the Leopoldstadt and guarded its bridges, as well as the Jewish Community Center on the other side of the Danube.[9] The experience of independence and self-sufficiency must have been exhilarating. But as normalcy returned, the larger plans of the activists came to nothing. To their surprise the new republic under its chancellor Karl Renner, only recently the Socialist party's theorist of national autonomy, opposed special rights for ethnic and religious minorities. The international situation developed less favorably than expected. Nor was the ideological en-

[9] The only printed reference to Bernfeld's command of the self-defense force that I have seen is in W. Hoffer's article, p. 158. The force itself and the Jewish Soldiers Councils, which incorporated men still in the service, are occasionally mentioned in the literature. See, for example, Robert Weltsch, "Österreichische Revolutionschronik," in *Der Jude*, iii, (1918–1919), p. 358: "Everywhere separate Jewish Soldiers Councils have been organized and have been put at the disposal of the Jewish National Councils. In Vienna the Jewish group was recognized by the city's commandant from the first days of the revolution on. . . . The Jewish population must admit that their sole protection are the Jewish soldiers who serve under the Jewish National Council."

thusiasm of the Jewish youth long sustained. *Jerubbaal* ceased publication; and the political energies that for a few months appeared so promising subsided into their ordinary meandering channels.

Bernfeld responded to these disappointments, in his view caused largely by human ignorance and helplessness, by writing a book and opening a school. In *The Jewish People and its Youth* he outlined a system of education in a classless society, in which the school became a central concern of the entire community. His proposals show similarities to the educational practices of some of the kibbutzim, which, indeed, Bernfeld influenced both by his writings and through his work in the *Paedagogium*.[10] The book is dedicated to Maria Montessori, the Berlin school teacher Berthold Otto, and to his associate in the prewar youth movement Gustav Wyneken.[11] Its arguments were also inspired by G. Stanley Hall's research into the feelings of children and adolescents, and especially by Freud, though in 1919 Bernfeld had not yet decided to become a psychoanalyst. It was not the medical aspect of psychoanalysis, Hoffer writes, but the preventive one that Bernfeld developed in his book. "The former, based on psychopathology, is understood as referring to therapy or healing, while prevention demands positive measures, so that illness and the necessity for healing will not arise. But it is not as simple as that, if one understands and applies Freud's psychology to education. Bernfeld had learned from Freud,

[10] W. Hoffer, *op. cit.*, pp. 166–167. See also Shmuel Nagler, "Psychotherapie im Rahmen der Kollektiverziehung," in *Kollektiverziehung im Kibbutz*, ed. L. Liegle, Munich, 1971, p. 266.

[11] Although Bernfeld's scientific and psychoanalytic interests had taken him very far from Wyneken, he continued to regard him highly as an educator, to the point of sending his two daughters by his first marriage to Wyneken's coeducational residential school, the Free School Community Wickersdorf.

though Freud had never said it explicitly, as I try to do here, that psychopathological development during childhood and adolescence is—within limits, of course—normal, though in no way harmless or negligible. It is difficult to convey the meaning of that statement comprehensively. What is meant can be compared with the infectious diseases of childhood; they too are harmless, normal, and we take them for granted; but we also know that measles or mumps can lead to disastrous complications from the child's point of view. Still, we welcome them, because they bring about a considerable degree of immunity for later life. It is not the same, but also not too different, when we think of the 'normal psychopathology' of childhood and adolescence. Therefore Bernfeld's conception of education covered this aspect of psychopathology, and prevention meant to him reacting to and providing for the child's normal psychopathology in the right and not in the wrong way. With a conception like that, Bernfeld was and still is far ahead of the overall conception of 'preventive' education as it was and still is generally understood." [12]

Bernfeld attempted to put his ideas both on preventive and therapeutic education into practice in a residential school for 240 "proletarian" war orphans, between the ages of three and sixteen, which he established in 1919 in five former military barracks. Anna Freud calls *Kinderheim Baumgarten* "a first experiment to apply psychoanalytic principles to education." [13] Bernfeld and his colleagues tried to help rather than control the children, their psychological difficulties were explored not suppressed, student self-government was attempted, and, despite all setbacks, one

[12] W. Hoffer, *op. cit.*, p. 161.
[13] Anna Freud, "Willi Hoffer," in *The Psychoanalytic Study of the Child*, xxiii (1968), London, p. 7.

of the teachers writes, "everybody who met these children after the first two or three months . . . would have agreed that these children were not 'institution children'." [14] It was hoped that *Baumgarten* would become a model for other residential schools; but Bernfeld fell seriously ill, and lack of sympathy with progressive education for workers' children on the part of the financial sponsors, the American Joint Distribution Committee, and incompetence among some of the administrative personnel, caused the school to close after six months.

"The disheartening experiences with this difficult venture," Anna Freud writes, "turned Bernfeld into a sceptic." [15] Despite his pronounced aptitude for organization, leadership, and politics, he turned away from institutions. Organizations, he wrote in his account of *Baumgarten*, are "vessels that can contain either poison or medicine"—what counted were the spirit, intelligence, and knowledge of the individual. [16] He ceased to take an active part in politics, and lost touch with Zionism, without ever relinquishing hope that a strong Jewish state would emerge in Palestine. Nor did he continue teaching as a regular activity. An attempt in 1931 to gain a university appointment came to nothing. But he was a frequent guest lecturer in progressive schools, and still spent much of his time working with teachers, writing, lecturing, and participating in conferences on educational topics. His main concern now was with psychoanalysis. He became a nonmedical analyst, and soon a training analyst in the psychoanalytic institutes of Vienna and Berlin, with a special interest in the psychology

[14] W. Hoffer, *op. cit.*, p. 165.
[15] Freud, p. 7.
[16] *Kinderheim Baumgarten: Bericht über einen ernsthaften Versuch mit neuer Erziehung*, Berlin, 1921, p. 48.

of children and adolescents. In 1925 appeared his pioneering study on the psychology of the infant.[17] In the same year he also published *Sisyphus*, a serious *jeu d'esprit*, the result of reflecting on his experiences in education, now structured and interpreted by psychoanalytic insight.

In the 1920's psychoanalytic writing on social and cultural issues was even more concerned than it is today with exposing the subjective nature of prevailing standards and conventions, a tendency that was reinforced in *Sisyphus* by the egalitarian convictions of its author. Education in modern Europe he regarded as an unattractive amalgam of capitalist interests and parental anxieties. But, typically, he was not blinded by the battle. Even as he refused to accept the class differences that, inevitably, accompanied the educational ideal of German neo-humanism, he loved and honored its unique intellectual vitality.

His general theory of education gave depth and balance to his attacks on the modern school, without lessening their immediate impact. Education, he argued, was at all times conservative, always devoted to the preservation of the status quo. Although it was our duty to eradicate the present inequities, we had no right to suppose that education in the socialist societies of the future would be rid of all injustice and conflict. The interaction of the means of production with biopsychological elements—a relationship susceptible to external change—significantly affected the individual; but basically all human beings were subject to the same psychological forces. Thus the limits of education could be found not only in a given political system, and in all political systems, but in the psychology of the child, of the adult, and of that variant of adulthood—the teacher.

[17] *Psychologie des Säuglings*, Vienna, 1925. A mediocre English translation was published in New York four years later.

Their internal barriers to healthy development could be reduced only through the better understanding of human instincts and functions that resulted from the investigations that psychoanalysis was pursuing with increasingly rigorous scientific methods. The psychoanalytic passages of *Sisyphus*, it may be worth noting, are of a concreteness and precision not always found in the literature. No doubt, if Bernfeld were writing today he would accompany his exposition of the importance of the child's healthy resolution of the oedipal conflict with a discussion of earlier developmental factors. Since 1925 much more has been learned about pre-oedipal difficulties, their effect on the way the child moves into the oedipal phase (or sometimes fails to do so) and especially about the development of the ego's capacities to work through the various stages of early childhood. But while the psychoanalytic argument might be expanded, there is no need to correct it, and it is presented with a clarity that is as admirable as the firmness with which the emotions of teachers and students are linked to their economic and political environment. Bernfeld was of course far from denying that limits also existed to psychoanalytic achievement. But at least if teachers came to appreciate the psychological forces in their students, in themselves, and in society, they might—in the words of one of Bernfeld's own students—grow aware "of their own frailties and the societal influences under which they work and be able not to be entirely swayed by them."[18]

Views such as these were equally distasteful to the doctrinaires of the right and the left, with the former deriving an added incentive for their rejection from the gusto with which the author brandished the name of the great Marx.

[18] Edith Buxbaum, "Three Great Psychoanalytic Educators," *The Reiss-Davis Clinic Bulletin*, iii, no. 1 (Spring, 1966), p. 7.

But Bernfeld's Marxism was of the kind that is more useful to intellectual effort than to party politics. The communist variety of Marxism in particular at first disappointed and then disgusted him. On the other hand, he owed to Marx the ability to identify the economic motives in history and society, even in such idealistically garbed phenomena as education. He was captivated by the taboo-destroying aspects of Marxist analysis, and in numerous lectures and articles he explored the affinity of Marxist and Freudian methods and dialectic.[19] The position of psychoanalysis in the Soviet Union was a matter of special interest to him. In 1932 he delivered his final judgment on their uneasy relationship in a long article that at the same time gave his opinions on other features of Marxism that had occupied him for two decades or more. The occasion for the article was the debate in psychoanalytic circles over Wilhelm Reich's attempts to combine Marxist ideology and psychoanalytic theory, which ended with Reich leaving psychoanalysis. Bernfeld accused Reich of passing off his private ideal of a world without limitations on the sexual drive as the goal of psychoanalysis, and attacked his effort to make analysis acceptable to the Russians by restricting its scope to the individual patient while excluding it from the study of social and political issues. This position, which was shared by such Russian supporters of psychoanalysis as J. Sapir, was deemed "entirely unacceptable" by the author of *Sisyphus*, if only, he wrote, because for the first time ever psychoanalysis gave men the opportunity of studying scientifically at least some of the areas that so far had been the domain of philosophy: social, religious, and cultural insti-

[19] Representative examples are "Psychoanalyse und Sozialismus," in *Der Kampf*, 1925; and the proceedings of a Berlin conference he chaired on "Sozialismus und Psychoanalyse," published in *Der sozialistische Arzt*, ii, nos. 2/3 (1927).

tutions, political movements, intellectual and artistic creation.[20] Bernfeld's criticism of Reich was interwoven with attacks on Soviet conditions, though he distinguished between individual scientists who tried to approach their tasks with objectivity and such representatives of the Party line as W. Jurinetz, whose work Bernfeld called "characteristic of the frighteningly superficial, journalistically crude manner, undisturbed by professional expertise, in which Communist science is not infrequently carried on today."[21] Not Marx was responsible for this perversion, but the *Vulgärmarxismus* of the Communists. "The error . . . that makes possible so much nonsense within Communist Marxism . . . rests in the arbitrary and false equation of philosophy and science."[22] Bernfeld adds that seven years earlier, in *Sisyphus*, he had already made plain his Marxist conviction that "all *practical* applications of a science would be shaped—even against the scientist's knowledge and wish—by the extrascientific tendencies and forces of society."[23] But scientific research itself must not be disturbed by value judgments, though the scientist's feelings and thoughts will naturally be influenced by his environment. In Russia, however, "restrictions on scientific enquiry . . . appear as soon as a scientific discipline makes statements that are in conflict with the existing system and its economic tendencies, or even that simply seem to be in

[20] "Die kommunistische Diskussion um die Psychoanalyse und Reichs Widerlegung der Todestriebhypothese," *Internationale Zeitschrift für Psychoanalyse*, xviii, no. 3 (1932), p. 374.

[21] *Ibid.*, p. 355. My translation cannot claim to have caught the full measure of scorn of the German original: "die erschreckend oberflächliche, von keiner Sachkenntniss getrübte, leitartikelartigverwilderte Art, in der nicht selten heutigentags kommunistische Wissenschaft getrieben wird."

[22] *Ibid.*, pp. 356, 362.

[23] *Ibid.*, pp. 376–377, note 12. The following quotation is from pp. 367–368.

conflict with them. . . . A kind of philosophy tests all scientific statements for their conformity with the political and economic system before discussing their accuracy. More radically and openly than anyone the Communists observe this principle (which among the European Communist parties . . . degenerates into cynical flexibility)." The Communists countered by branding Bernfeld a supporter of capitalism, or classed him among the "Austro-Marxist school reformers" with their "sham-revolutionary pedagogic idealism," whose educational improvements only helped prolong bourgeois society and the oppression of proletarian children. Bernfeld's response was that at least one of the children's burdens, "lack of access to proper education, could be lightened by educational work of the kind that he himself was doing."[24]

From the second half of the 1920's on, Bernfeld's preoccupation with the psychology of the young and with education was gradually superseded by studies on psychoanalytic theory, the biological roots of analysis, and quantification. The interest he had always shown in biology and mathematics strengthened his long-standing wish to broaden the scientific basis of psychoanalysis and to explore

[24] "Freedom or organization?" anonymous review of two volumes of Bernfeld's collected writings and of a new edition of *Grundfragen der proletarischen Erziehung* by Edwin Hoernle, the German Communists' chief spokesman on education in the 1920's, in the *Times Literary Supplement*, 12 February 1970. See also the front-page article, presumably by the same author who is far from being an unqualified admirer of Freud, "When dogma bites dogma, or the difficult marriage of Marx and Freud," *T. L. S.*, 8 January 1971, a knowledgeable and witty discussion of seven works dealing with social and political aspects of psychoanalysis, including the third volume of the edition of Bernfeld's writings reviewed the year before. This three-volume edition is an unauthorized collection printed by a publisher primarily known for his list of radical ephemera and pornography. A brief epilogue by Lutz von Werder and Reinhart Wolff tries to claim Bernfeld as a spiritual comrade-in-arms of West Germany's New Left.

possibilities of interaction with other disciplines. After he settled in the United States in 1937 it opened yet another area of research to him: the study of Freud's scientific beginnings, which resulted in a series of much admired essays that combined biography with the history of science. But his last paper, written a few months before his death in 1953, returned once more to questions of education. In a talk given before the San Francisco Psychoanalytic Society, he protested against the bureaucratization of modern psychoanalytic training, speculated on possibilities of less formal ways of teaching men to be competent therapists, and called on his listeners to be more critical about their behavior as teachers and students of psychoanalysis. An ironic, realistic appraisal of things as they are, coupled with a perhaps utopian declaration that they do not need to be like that, the paper was *Sisyphus* in miniature, addressed to the special problems of professional education.[25]

In recent years renewed interest is being shown in Bernfeld's work. *Sisyphus* and other of his writings have been reprinted; French, Spanish, and Italian translations have appeared or are under way; and a German edition of his essays on Freud, originally written in English, is being prepared. In part his new popularity may be due to the strange eagerness with which radical groups in Europe and America scour the past for respectable historical ancestors. But as I have suggested, Bernfeld is an uncomfortable ally in ideological slanging matches. Surely he is being read again for better reasons. The cultural and political milieu in which he worked has proved of particular interest and value to this generation, and the problems of education that he discussed continue to be with us today. The solutions he of-

[25] "On Psychoanalytic Training, *The Psychoanalytic Quarterly,* xxxi (1962).

fered—though he would have smiled at the phrase—had little to do with developing new methods, and even less with taking "power" from one group in the school and giving it to another; but a great deal with the understanding of people's feelings and emotions. That understanding—even if achieved on a vast scale—will never lead to perfect harmony: the differences in knowledge, in age, in motives that nearly always characterize the encounter between teacher and student are too great. A working relationship between irreconcilables, Bernfeld might have said, is all we should hope for. Or, as he put it himself more precisely (in *Kinderheim Baumgarten*, p. 52) and with his marvellous sense for the dynamics of learning: "No theory of education can resolve the antinomy between the justified will of the child and the justified will of the teacher; on the contrary, education consists in this antinomy."

Peter Paret

Peter Paret is Professor of European History at Stanford.

Translator's Note

This essay was written in a style that confronted the translator with special difficulties. Its insights and perceptions are presented with an air of informality and improvisation, leading to frequent interruption of the exposition and argument by digressions, asides, and strongly affective personal statements. It was clear to me that a literal translation would try the American reader's patience and perhaps cause him to lose the thread of the ideas set forth. I have therefore compressed some passages, deleted a few, divided and simplified involved sentences, reset paragraphs, and eliminated a number of possible obscurities and inconsistencies. None of these affects the substance or the spirit of the original work. Some footnotes, most of them biographical, have been added to the text. I am indebted to Professor and Mrs. Paret for refinements in the psychoanalytical passages of the book.

Frederic Lilge

I

On the Theory and Philosophy
of Education

In her *Reminiscences of Froebel* the Baroness Marenholz-Bülow[1] tells of her efforts to win the active support of von Wydenbruch, the Weimar Minister of Education, for Froebel's kindergarten. In the course of several dinner conversations with the Minister she tried to dispel the objections that had been brought to his attention and spoke eloquently of the freedom for which men would be educated by Froebel's method. The Minister seemed inclined to grant such a possibility, but freedom itself did not appear to him desirable. Indeed, the very word was dangerous for the year was 1850. The baroness hastened to assure him that she meant only inner freedom, the freedom to develop one's personality. Von Wydenbruch doubted that Froebel's method could achieve this aim because human nature would remain what it had always been, imperfect. Still, he

[1] Bertha von Marenholz-Bülow (1816–1893) was a dedicated and highly effective champion of Friedrich Froebel, the pioneer of nursery education in Germany. By her writings, travels, and personal contacts with influential people she helped establish the kindergarten in German states and in England, France, Holland, Belgium, Switzerland, and Italy. Her *Erinnerungen an Froebel* was translated by Mary Mann, the widow of the educational reformer Horace Mann, and published in Boston in 1877.—*Tr.*

promised that at a more propitious time he would not neglect to do what he could to promote Froebel's method.
For the present it was necessary to establish law and order
in the German states.

I have chosen this anecdote as an introduction because it
condenses and symbolizes ideas which seem to me important to the discussions that lie ahead. It directs us through
opposing points of view to the criteria that I believe are central to any discussion of the limits of education. To begin
with, we encounter the benign skepticism of the experienced statesman toward the promises of educational theory.
To be sure, he is kind, perhaps not only because it is a lady,
and a baroness at that, who describes Froebel's odd ideas to
him, but also because he is sympathetic to the basic aims, at
least in so far as these aims have the sympathies of all mankind. Were he incapable of sharing such feelings, he would
have to regard himself with suspicion and contempt. Thus,
he either remains unconscious of not really sharing those
sympathies, or he is careful not to betray his inner resistance
to the ideals of the noble Froebel. In the case of diplomats
one can't be sure. Other types of men might honestly feel:
how wonderful it would be if . . . The Minister, however,
has no faith in the possibility of realizing what perhaps is
intrinsically beautiful and desirable. He knows too well the
endless chain of insurmountable difficulties that obstruct
even the most modest changes in human institutions and
relations. He is no stranger to the impenetrable complexity
of reality, and both history and his own experience have
taught him to reckon with the grotesque disparity that exists between effort and achievement in human affairs. Froebel seems to him to have inverted this relationship. The
Minister simply cannot believe that human nature and institutions can be radically changed by a little singing and

play because he knows that even prodigious and consuming labors produce at best only minimal results.

I probably overestimate the historic Herr von Wydenbruch, but it does not matter. We are not concerned here with him and the year 1850, but rather with his attitude toward educational theory and educators because it is symbolic of public opinion even today. This attitude, shared by the thoughtful and the thoughtless alike, combines a tolerance for the ideals of education with a resolute and cold disbelief in its programs, means, and promises. The only notable exception to this are the educators themselves. The reader may be inclined to think I exaggerate, and point out that since the war [of 1914–1918] broad sections of the public have taken a lively interest in education. Educational issues now engage the attention of groups that are not professionally concerned with them. Few principles meet with such universal agreement as that the problems of the present, as well as the fate of the future, can only be settled with the help of education.

One may grant this interest, but one should not, overestimate it. Two factors operate to conceal the true situation. First, a large group of laymen vitally interested in education consists of parents. They frequently have reason to be dissatisfied with the development of their children and therefore look about for counsel, diagnosis, and prognosis. The educative role of the family is now everywhere in question, and the old pedagogical remedies on which our grandparents still relied have ceased to be effective, or at least have lost most of their authority. With regard to moral and social questions, a general insecurity prevails, robbing parents of the courage to enforce their will and lay down the law. Beset by a host of feelings, which include guilt and hostility to family and children, parents are caught in a

3

situation of psychic stress and reach out for whatever help tested educational doctrines may give them. Even if these should not quite bring the desired results, they would at least permit the parents to justify themselves: they could say that they had done what was possible.

This situation indeed creates a considerable interest in education, but not necessarily a high appreciation of it. On the contrary, there are indications that predict an early fatigue and disappointment on the part of the parents. For the plain fact is that educational theory does not meet the expectations people set on it. It gives no clear, unambiguous, concrete directions. Its methods rarely assure success. Its prognosis—often false and never reliable—points forever to a remote, incalculable future. If despite these failings no rapid decline of interest can be observed, the reason simply is that for every parent who drops out, either from disappointment or because his children have grown up, a younger one takes his place. Thus, the existing need for and interest in educational theory does not produce a truer appreciation of it: its authority is not recognized, its rules are not observed and its representatives do not rise in social esteem. All that is accomplished is a masking of the prevailing skepticism and disparagement.

A second factor helping to obscure the situation is even more important. It will occupy us at some length later and I mention it only briefly here. The educational system with all its institutions is outmoded and in need of reform. The recent rapid changes in politics, economics, and society require determined efforts to adapt the educational system to them. Since many forces are at work trying to frustrate such reforms, the progressives must fight for them and enlist the public's interest for their cause. Unfortunately, the public has only a limited grasp of the values at stake in this struggle. Its interest extends only to such issues as the replacement of objectionable pedagogical relics by newer institutions that may perhaps prove useful, but at any rate will work no harm. For example, people get stirred up over the fight against the classical secondary school because they regard it as noxious, antiquated, and detrimental to contemporary needs. Yet these same people may declare educational theory to be quite useless, its goals impractical and its methods ineffective.

It is understandable that the educators are not quite capable of viewing this situation objectively. They take themselves and their work too seriously for that. Indeed, as the Wydenbruchs hold, they overrate it. But why should we begrudge the educators, any more than metalworkers, gardeners, or physicians, the pride they take in their work, or object to their professional bias of deeming it more important than other, equally productive work? We all overestimate what we love while we reproach others for the same failing. In educators, however, this self-esteem is more than the common professional bias for it assumes forms and contents that are exciting and momentous: what the baroness promises in Froebel's name is nothing less than the salvation of mankind. Yet opposite her sit the men of the world who listen, smile coldly, and prevent the promised salvation. Surely this is no small matter. It must be possible to determine whether Froebel is right. We are not asking whether his ideas are noble and desirable, but whether they can be realized. At least we need to know whether there is some criterion by which this question can be resolved one way or another. Were Froebel proved right, the skeptical Minister would cease to appear the man of experience and worldly wisdom and stand revealed as the enemy. If, however, the Minister were right and Froebel's promises, along

5

with his entire theory, proved false, the conclusion would be more ominous. Not only would the educators then have to withdraw their claims or face ridicule, the whole educational theory would have to submit to a reexamination that comes close to an indictment. For it would be suspected of having wasted an immense expenditure of effort, time, and money, frustrated the happiness of children, and deceived their parents. The possibility looms that educational theory may prevent the very future it promises.

If educational theory is to be cleared of these grave charges, it will have to submit to a trial in which the case against it will be argued with a certain bias. It should not complain about this, for if it emerges with a favorable verdict, its position will be stronger. I will permit myself, therefore, to adopt in the ensuing inquiry some of the skepticism, irony, and even hostility that echo in the pessimistic words of the Minister. But it would not do to surrender to that mood. Although his conversation reveals the profound disbelief and suspicion of all noneducators, at the same time it also makes us suspicious of this sort of person. Herr von Wydenbruch does not believe in Froebel's method. But if he did, he would suppress it all the same because its aims are dangerous and mean nothing less than revolution. What if the Minister's skepticism were unfounded? He and his kind would then be responsible for the fact that the great and eternal aims remain unfulfilled and that men are what they are because they are prevented from becoming better. This is precisely what educational philosophers assert.

It is odd that a question of such moment and urgency should still be undecided and that the common response to it should continue to consist of reproaches and suspicion. Suppose medicine were in the situation in which education

6

still finds itself; for example, that someone claimed to have found a cure for cancer. An extensive scientific apparatus would at once be put to work to decide the worth of the claim, and its decision would carry authority. The theory of education lacks such legitimate and authoritative criteria. It is still in its first tentative phase and its further development into a science of education faces powerful opposition. It has no clear conception of itself, and a general willingness to think about educational matters in scientific terms does not exist. The question as to what the limits of education *are*, whether the Froebels or the Wydenbruchs are *right*, is a scientific one, and it must be decided independently of the aims, desires, and intentions of the opposing parties.

Education almost alone among social and cultural activities lacks this scientific attitude. It seems to be at the stage of development that medicine occupied when the treatment of disease and the science of medicine were still independent of each other, or when medical science did not yet exist. Even in those days illnesses were treated, and sometimes even cured. Treatment goes back to the dawn of time: a reaction of the human being to strange, painful, threatening phenomena of his body, which sometimes succeeded in removing the dangerous condition. But the methods of this primitive, animistics medicine had nothing to do with the success of the treatment. Specific measures were haphazardly motivated and determined, and for some unempirical reason trust in their healing effects was attached to them. Failure did not diminish faith in the treatment, because independent of all empirical proof the treatment satisfied the psychological needs that had given rise to it—superstitions perhaps, religious tendencies, or unconscious guilt feelings. Certainly the method of treatment had specific causes, but not the pretended purpose of healing the illness. To give an example in which medicine and education touch on one another: in most primitive societies, and even among peasants of advanced societies, the teething of children is thought of as an extremely dangerous process. The child must be guarded against its threats, and countless rites are carefully and anxiously observed when the child approaches this painful period in its development. Some are quite strange, for example the custom reported in Styria: when the child begins to teethe, its mother must bite off the head of a live mouse, and tie this head on a silk thread around her child's neck. Science has taught us that teething is safe, and that its progress is not dependent on the fate of mice. If the purpose of the rite was really the protection of the child then thousands of mice needlessly sacrificed head and life. Who can say how many medical and educational methods, which—in all innocence and hope—we observe today, are equally pointless, if less conspicuous? Medicine arises out of the formulation, execution, and modification of such activities. It seeks to rationalize action in accord with its healing purpose. Any action that does not achieve or support this purpose is judged to be in error, to be superstitious, regardless how many other purposes it may satisfy. Compared to animistic healing, contemporary medicine is highly rational. In all areas contemporary society is more rational than any earlier society.

But education is one of the activities that remains least affected by the process of rationalization. Education, like healing, is as old as the human race, older indeed because animals too exhibit social processes that can only be interpreted as education. Scattered reflections and expressions about this or that fact of education, both descriptive and normative, are also ancient. But the growth of such reflections in scope, depth, and coherence is very gradual. Only imperfectly and rather late in the history of a culture are they organized into a theory of education and obtain a determining influence on educational practice. A fairly comprehensive theory appears in Europe only in the second half of the eighteenth century, preceded by more limited attempts directed at such special areas as the *ratio studendi* of the universities, instruction in elementary schools, the education of princes and of noble youth to which both Locke and Rousseau basically addressed themselves.

The meaning and function of educational theory is to make educational practice rational. But its authority to effect this rationalization is undeveloped and weak. Moreover, the theory contains even in its rudimentary state an element that imperils the rationalization of educational practice, and the cause is to be found in the short but dubious history of educational theory.

The advance of rationalization, which one may call progress, is accomplished in two steps. The first of these is the intellectual achievement of an individual; the second, a change in the behavior of many and potentially of all men. Comenius invented the picture book; millions of teachers, mothers, and others then employed it in place of whatever was in use before. The intellectual achievement requires of its author the courage to emancipate himself from tradition and the imagination to think of something new. Since this educational innovation is also related to what goes on in society, the author must accomplish a third aim: he must replace the mode of thought he discards with another that is expedient and functional in the sense of serving a purpose. For pedagogy is not poetry, it is rational thought. An educational innovation is added to the body of educational

9

theory only if it accords with the basic trend toward rationalization that is inherent in all social activity. This is not meant as a value judgment, but as a criterion that can help us make a simple distinction.

Whereas the reputation of a mathematician or a poet is fully defined by his individual achievement, that of an educator is not. His work is part of the social fabric, and it requires a following if it is not to remain incomplete. What determines a successful completion is the authority, charisma, or plain achievement of the author himself. If he wields power, he can compel the abolition of traditional usage and the adoption of his innovation. Or an established power may take possession of it and do it for him, which has frequently been the fate of the great educators. Again, if the innovation is accepted voluntarily first by small and then by larger groups, its propagation will be the more rapid the stronger its support by some established authority, say religion, or the deeper the effect of the author's personal charisma. In the final analysis, however, success depends upon the nature of the achievement itself, that is, upon its utility. We touch here upon complex relations and interactions that belong to the sociology of education, a field of inquiry that hardly exists as yet. But it would appear that educational theory has fulfilled its function less than its present scope leads one to expect. The reason for this failure we will attempt to find first and foremost in the history of educational theory and its authors. Evidently, some deficiency in power, authority, charisma, or truth does exist here.

It may be objected that my line of argument is wrongheaded. The history of education, it will be said, proves that a wide gap between educational theory and practice does not exist and that both have shown gratifying and uninterrupted progress—even though educational practice, being the more difficult of the two, may have lagged behind a little. To advance my argument beyond this point, I must insist upon terminological precision. We commonly distinguish between instruction and education and, correspondingly, between the theory of instruction and the theory of education.[2] But, paradoxically, though none will dispute this distinction, all neglect to observe it. People talk about education when in fact they think exclusively in terms of instruction, thus mistaking a part for the whole. The entire system of education is host to many other disciplines besides the theory and methodology of instruction. Yet this alone receives comfortable, even luxurious, accommodations whereas all the rest are condemned to languish in a dark corner. I do not begrudge methodology its high standard of living, but I want the theory of education to have a grand development so that the proportions between the parts and the whole are restored.

All the same, one particular aspect of instructional methodology is worthy of note. Granted, the reputation of the professionals in this area does not extend beyond a narrow circle of experts, nor are any of them blessed with the charisma and human greatness we meet among the more important educators. Nevertheless, methodology exceeds all the rest of educational theory in effectiveness since it more

[2] The German terms are *Didaktik* and *Pädagogik*. The first covers a broad range of interests that include theories of teaching and learning, the psychology and methodology of teaching the various school subjects, and theories of curriculum construction Since the author looks upon *Didaktik* as a technology of education, it has been translated as theory and methodology of instruction or, when warranted by the text, as psychology of instruction. The second, *Pädagogik*, has been rendered as theory and philosophy of education, but the term pedagogy is also used because it is briefer, even though it has never fully established itself in the professional language of education.—*Tr.*

nearly approaches the level of rationalization that generally obtains in our society. This effectiveness is enhanced because the methodologists have borrowed the authority of greater men like Comenius, Rousseau, and Pestalozzi. The work of these men, though not limited to the theory of instruction, laid the basis for and gave decisive, revolutionary impulses to it. Still, the help the methodologists received from those patron saints should not be overestimated, as the case of Pestalozzi illustrates. He was the kindest of men, a generous soul and an exceptional spirit, endowed with great healing and educative powers, who devoted half his life—half a century almost—to children. Truly revolutionary ideas and innovations were fathered by him, yet of all these only one found its way into educational practice. This was his methodology of elementary-school instruction. In itself perhaps of questionable validity, disfigured already by the first generation of disciples, and in his own view one of his lesser achievements, it was torn from the context of his whole work in which he himself wanted it to be judged. This has been the typical fate of the teachings of important educators, and it ought to make us think.

Evidently a theory of instruction need not depend for its success on the charisma of a creative individual, and it may become divorced from it. When this happens, the art of teaching seems to some people to be degraded to a mere technique and to sink in social rank to the level of, say, the art of raising and keeping bees. The derision here implied is quite inappropriate because teaching methods can take their place among the means that serve to transform irrational customs and usages into rational procedures. Teaching has clearly defined tasks whose performance is controllable: certain subject matters must be taught to certain age groups within definite time allotments. Teaching thus meets the general conditions that must exist if progressive rationalization of any social activity is to take place. These specific tasks are performed by a professional group, membership in which does not require human or any other kind of greatness but does demand professional training in the methodology of instruction.

Educational philosophers and theorists do their utmost to becloud these plain and simple facts by insisting that teachers not merely instruct but also educate. Unlike teaching, educating is not a profession entrusted to a single group: numerous and various social forces have a share in it. Educational philosophers also fail to provide any criteria that would permit us to judge whether a child has been "educated," whereas it can easily be determined whether he has learned to read. Their insistence that schools not merely instruct but also educate might at least lead them to recognize that the schools, such as they are, make it impossible for teachers to be educators also. Instead of concluding that radical changes must be brought about in the institution in order that both functions may be fulfilled, the pedagogues merely reiterate their unreasonable demand.

There are teachers who, having chosen the profession from idealistic motives, sincerely wish they could meet that demand. But once they are in the system, social and economic reasons, which attract the mass of teachers in the first place, are added to the original idealism and eventually determine any person's career within the profession. Faced with the virtual impossibility to do more than instruct, the high-minded teachers are left with few alternatives. They may deceive themselves into believing they are molding young personalities in accordance with lofty educational ideals—which is easily done because teachers don't know what children think and do outside the classroom. They may worry, feel frustrated, despise themselves, and become embittered over the years. Or they may renounce all lofty ideals and resign themselves to being instructors and nothing more. But whatever inner personal adjustments a teacher makes, he must always pass the public professional test: he must be able to instruct effectively.

Society compels the teacher to deliver certain services at specified standards while being wholly indifferent to his individual dispositions and motives. Only the measurable achievement counts and is paid for. All the rest is the individual's affair and he is free to rejoice or despair over his work. The bluntness of this social requirement may of course be veiled. The introduction to a school catalogue may state that teachers are expected to educate moral and religious men—and then proceed to enumerate subjects and schedules. But it is not through the teaching profession that those values are realized. Moral and religious men existed in 1224 no less than in 1924 whereas, and this is the essential difference, the number of literate people then may perhaps equal the number of illiterates today. The god of society is neither hurt nor angry with his teachers, but smiles knowingly. They did their utmost, became frustrated, and despised themselves in the process. He really expected no more from them than the liquidation of illiteracy, but they aimed at the realization of the moral and religious man. Why deprive them of their illusion? If he did, they might not exert themselves at all, for a mere twelve hundred marks a year.

The distinction we made between education and instruction has led to the recognition that the latter has precise and controllable tasks for whose achievement an entire profession is held accountable. Hence instruction, along with the theory and methodologies that guide it, plays a part in the rationalization of the work of modern society. More-over, the theory of instruction appears as an empirical discipline. If, for example, a teacher asserted that the way to teach a certain rule is to make the student repeat it three times, sufficient evidence could be gathered to prove or disprove the assertion. Instructional theory may not be a science in the strict sense, but its procedures at least have some scientific ingredients. It aims at creating a body of valid insights concerning learning, motivation, and the like, and, generally speaking, it looks as though it were the exemplary discipline in education.

Unfortunately, an examination of the literature compels one to revise this high opinion. The discipline is devoid of nearly all the qualities and subtleties we have come to associate with scientific inquiry. One misses any sense of the complexity of reality, of the limitations of our methods, and of the human mind itself. The amount of effort expended on relatively simple matters seems excessive and arouses one's suspicion. Are reading, writing, arithmetic, and clay-modeling really such difficult arts as to require three folio volumes, with one hundred and twenty pages of bibliography, for an introduction alone? At the same time, one is shocked and appalled to learn that everything is made so terribly and ridiculously simple: half a dozen easy tests suffice to certify officially a child's mental age, the level of his development, his aptitude, and even his future. Something here protests in us, or are we letting our feelings bias our judgment?

I think it can be shown that the theory of instruction is afflicted with false modesty, and that the empirical and rational tendencies present in it are prematurely and arbitrarily arrested. It forgets that the educational system as it has emerged and changed continually in the last few centuries is a complex social accretion that produces conse-quences and effects of which the individual teacher's ac-tivity is but one. We cannot even say with any assurance how important his function in this system is. Yet the theory of instruction limits itself to this activity and indeed only to the conscious, mandate-oriented part of it. All the rest is ex-cluded from empirical examination and critical reflection. The framework of the prevailing school system is accepted as though divinely ordained so that the question of how the instructional process itself is affected by it cannot even be raised. Thus, the theory of instruction that guides the teacher's work restricts itself to a partial rationality while leaving undisturbed the whole system and the irrational forces that move and determine it.

Such omissions make it impossible to take the theory in its present state seriously. It needs to be supplemented by another discipline, something like a science of educational institutions, before it can attain the scope and authority of a theory capable of rethinking the system in its entirety and directing it in accordance with rational objectives. If this were accomplished, numerous conditions and practices ac-cepted blindly today would become questionable: the di-vision of children's lives between school and family or family substitutes, such as the street and the gang; uniform grouping by age; the definition of teaching objectives ac-cording to grade levels; and the quantitative allotment of the learning material to daily periods and school years.

It is necessary to remind ourselves that the institution we call school did not result from a rational attempt to realize the purposes of instruction. It existed before any theory of instruction and it remains opposed to it. The school has its origin in the economic, financial, and political forces of society and in the ideological requirements and cultural valuations that reflect those forces. It has its roots also in the nonrational views and valuations that are the unconscious product of the relations between the generations and of the prevailing class structure. Whatever direction these forces may take, they are more likely to deflect from than to aid the attainment of instructional objectives. At any rate, to leave such a possibility unexamined is not in keeping with the scientific attitude. The theory and psychology of instruction lack the courage and consistency of scientific endeavor.

Another and even harsher verdict would be pronounced upon it by a revolutionary pedagogy. From its point of view, the theory and psychology of instruction help to preserve the existing school system and to perpetuate thereby those vile educational effects that the system in reality produces upon generation after generation. These effects are not what the schools claim they are and they make a mockery of all educational doctrines, programs, decrees, meetings, and sermons. What educator or methodologist has the courage to admit this truth? Instead they proceed with their thinking, writing, and experimenting, unaware of the ridiculous situation in which they put themselves, and unable to perceive the futility of their misplaced efforts. Still, their work has at least the noxious effect of preserving the *status quo*.

Finally, I object to the content of the theory and psychology of instruction. The subject of its investigation is the product of its own foreshortened vision. It mistakes the psychic surface of the child for the whole child. Simply because the school separates learning from life and reduces vital beings to mere learners who are either bright or dull, the theory of instruction fancies that its findings about school learning represent true insights into learning generally and even into the life of the child. It assumes that the young mind is neatly organized into distinct faculties for reading, writing, arithmetic, manual arts, and religion; it then proceeds to investigate each and proclaims such rules as it is able to establish as psychological laws. It is blind to the integrity of the child's life, to his drives, desires, and ideals, and knows nothing of the pleasure or the hatred he feels for formal learning. I am not saying that it is useless to observe children under the tangled conditions of the school. Such experiments may prove instructive, though they would certainly be remote from life. One must know, however, what one is doing. But the methodologists of instruction, here as elsewhere, do not know. And that may the Lord forgive them, for I cannot.

This is my judgment of the seemingly exemplary part of pedagogy. I shall be hard pressed to do equal justice to the remainder, which is more extensive and held in greater esteem. As it is impossible to compress into a slender volume a comprehensive and searching analysis, I shall instead select from the mass of evidence a sufficient number of arguments and indictments and attempt to present them skillfully and pungently so as to intrigue and captivate the reader. Besides, in a situation where one believes onself surrounded by a wall of prejudice it would be difficult not to become diverted from the careful and just weighing of all the evidence. Only a certain impetuosity, so the author pleads, can keep him on his course.

Unlike its methodological auxiliary, the theory of education is in no sense or measure scientific. Less than a dozen little-known essays and no more than half that number of small obscure books perhaps exist that might contradict this preemptory statement. I shall take the liberty of ignoring them in order to simplify matters, for they are negligible items—hardly more than hesitant attempts at a beginning of a science of education. I shall also leave aside the history of education because it will concern us in another context. In all the rest—and here for an instant there flashes through my mind that revered Comenius Library, with its hundreds of thousands of volumes, in the solid city of Leipzig—there is not a breath of the spirit of science, whatever other values it may have.

Let us begin by paying tribute to the great figures, the pedagogues—admittedly an ugly term that unintentionally but rightly puts us on guard, detracting just a trifle from their claims to greatness. Let us confess our tender affection for Pestalozzi and Jean Paul, our awe of the rough, unbending Fichte, and a curious respect for the alarming Rousseau, so productive and ingenious in his derangement. We are touched, too, by Salzmann's idyll at Schnepfenthal, for which we may feel just a twinge of envy and longing; and even Basedow, promoter that he was, is surely more than a cause for our amusement.[3] Going farther back still, we meet Comenius's kind, intelligent eyes that spanned the entire *orbis pictus* and peer at us from a face of bearded dignity. There is a host of others, known today only to scholars, to whom we are bound by similar feelings of respect and reverence. However, our purpose here is not to honor these men, to pay them courtesies, and least of all to treat them

[3] Jean Paul, pen name of J. P. F. Richter (1763–1825), author of eccentric novels, also wrote a treatise on education entitled *Levana* (1807). J. G. Fichte (1762–1814), best known as a philosopher of German idealism, also concerned himself with national education and university reform. J. B. Basedow (1724–1790) established his Philantropinum at Dessau in 1774, and C. G. Salzmann (1744–1811) conducted a new type of school at Schnepfenthal, founded in 1784. By their practical and literary work the two last-named men propagated a nonclassical, utilitarian style of education.—*Tr.*

with indulgence. A rough critical treatment can no longer harm them, but it may perhaps benefit their teachings. Besides, confound it, how would they have treated me, had I so much as stirred between, say, 1650 and 1850!

To begin with, the work of many influential educators lacks an empirical base. Rousseau, for example, related to children throughout his life as a reluctant father or a casual observer. The theories of Fichte, Herbart, Basedow and Jean Paul rest upon a pitifully small experience gathered during a few years' employment as private tutors. Such men are like astronomers who sleep at night and by day let others tell them of the stars. Their knowledge of children was negligible, gained through hearsay or in a small group of personal acquaintances. Reliance on introspection and remembrance, too, is of dubious value. Anyone who thinks about childhood and youth comes under the sway of affective forces that impair objective thought: his image of himself as a child inevitably obtrudes. This image is the unconscious medium through which our personal experience of other children passes and by which it is marred and impaired. Moreover, the remembrance of our own childhood, so vivid and intrusive and which we appear to hold in good faith, is nothing like the faithful reproduction of an object. It is rather a profoundly biased force, whose origin lies in the obscure depths of our psyche, to which we cling and with which we arm ourselves lifelong against powerful enemies within. From this crucial struggle, in which the aim justifies all means, truth and knowledge can hardly be expected to emerge.

The conscious recollection of our childhood consists of isolated elements of actual experiences whose connectedness has been broken up by repression. Such recollection takes place in adolescence when definitive ego formations occur, and the method employed resembles that of ruthless autocracy. Whatever does not agree with the masterplan, whatever does not fit into the desired image, is destroyed. For the new ego ideal turns against the whole childhood and is able to accept but little of childish modes of feeling, thinking and acting. It is the very purpose of the new personality structure to overcome and, if possible, to annihilate that earlier phase of life. Such isolated elements as do remain are reconnected and supplemented by a revised version of the actual past. In the intensity of this revision something new arises which, compared to the truth that has been destroyed, is more like poetry.[4] I am not referring to the external facts of life, though these too are not exempt from being touched up, but to its internal psychic structure. This is erected upon a ground of which all trace has disappeared, the first years of life being totally forgotten. If part of that period is restored to consciousness, we find that those original experiences determine the hidden master plan that controls the use of all residual memories. These are now employed in such a way as to conceal areas of the most intense psychic conflict from the consciousness and to make unrecognizable all facts that contradict the consciously remembered image. Clearly, this distorted reconstruction of one's own childhood cannot serve as a basis for true insight. Yet educational theories have held such a naive conception of childhood.

It was not their only error. We should not forget that the victims of repression are passionate infantile desires and urges, and it is these the naive view of childhood covers over. But these urges and desires are imperishable. They endure a thousand repressions and, though altered in shape

[4] An allusion to Goethe's autobiography *Dichtung und Wahrheit.*—Tr.

and aim, ineluctably press towards satisfaction. The educators themselves do not escape this inevitability even as they think and write about their subject. One of them, guided solely by the knowledge of his own childhood but repressing its passionate and violent urges, arrives at the glorification of childhood and celebrates it as the ideal human condition. "Everything is good as it comes from the hands of the creator," he writes, and so places a value upon the result of repression while simultaneously satisfying the repressed urges. Infantile aggression against the adult suppressors still rages but finds a new expression, to wit: "Everything degenerates under the hands of men."

Another of the authors we mentioned appears to have labored hard to control the impulses that conflicted with his ego ideal by repressing them. His childhood recollection consists only of a few harmlessly malicious pranks but a harsh lesson is derived from the Pyrrhic victory he won over his own impulses: "Discipline your children and bend them early to your will. Parents who neglect this and allow their children to grow up like rank weeds do not deserve to be called animals, let alone men." In this case infantile aggression is aimed at children, including his own.

The naive conception of childhood we have tried to illumine and to criticize determines not only the personal views of educational authors, it also inhabits their educational system. The presence there of unconscious, uncontrollable emotions constitutes the most telling evidence against the presumed objectivity of educational theories. Some may grant this to be true and yet arrive at an opposite value judgment. All this proves, they would object, is that the teachings of the great educators owe infinitely more to intuition than to cogitation. I agree, and this is precisely what I have been asserting. Their writings possess high esthetic and moral value. Some give us pleasure, others move us profoundly and may convert us to their ideas. And being intuitions, they arise from the deep unconscious and in turn touch the reader there. They affect us like art, poetry, and philosophy which, in fact, they are—but this should be read as a descriptive statement, not as a necessarily positive valuation. Some pedagogical doctrines are good and others are bad poetry. But to ask whether a poem rests upon verifiable experience or whether it is true is nonsensical, for the criteria of science do not apply.

I now have my objectors boxed in. The achievements of the great pedagogues are intuitive products of art, they are not science. Valued as poetry, they may rank high, but by the same token their value as science will be low. The question is, however, whether they want to be and should be valued as poetry. To have to ask that question only shows how disagreeable the situation really is. To digress for a moment, it is as though the sculptor of the Zeus at Otricoli had promised to create a living god who can scowl and throw thunderbolts with his marble arm. Standing before this artistic marvel, feeling its power and admiring its beauty, we forget that promise and forgive the artist for not achieving his aim because we perceive the fulfillment of something greater. But the stone god remains dead, the sculptor told a lie. The analogy applies to the pedagogical doctrines or poems we are discussing. Every one of them makes statements about reality. It predicts or promises that if its methods are adopted, children will grow up into those ideal men we mentioned at the beginning of this essay. Such statements and promises are the essence of the whole doctrine, without which it would not exist at all. And because of such a promise, a pedagogical system is, objectively, not poetry though subjectively that may be its origin and the way it affects us. Its value depends solely on whether the promise can be fulfilled. Only then is the doctrine true.

I sense an objection in the reader's mind that I must refute lest I be suspected of carelessness. So I hasten to say that I am aware that several great pedagogues founded and conducted schools, in places that have since become historic, such as Dessau, Stanz, Iverdün, Keilhau and Schnepfenthal. There, as some would remind me, hundreds of children of all kinds lived and learned under the observant eyes of the respective educator. There doctrines were tested and an empirical base did exist. I grant that the naive notion of childhood those educators entertained was corrected by the manifold experience gathered in their schools. This is reflected, for example, in the concrete and vivid language in which Pestalozzi writes about children, which compares favorably with the abstract schemes of Fichte or the emotional distortions of Rousseau. However, even in men like Pestalozzi a tendency toward *a priori* assertiveness remains, and this would not change even if their experiential base had been infinitely broader. For the empirical basis of our observations, indispensable though it may be, is not of decisive importance; it is our scientific attitude that determines the necessary corrections and limitations of our preconceptions. The science of education asks how children behave, not how they affect the observer. But the great pedagogues of history are concerned with how and what they feel toward children, with emotions such as love, pity, hope, disgust and horror. They do not see the child as it is but only the relationship that exists between it and themselves. Even if they were able to leave themselves out of it, the question as to what the child is in and by itself still would not interest them because their sole concern is how to transform it into something else. To them the child is a means to some theological, ethical, or utopian end.

Lacking the scientific attitude, pedagogues of the past were unable to make proper use of their practical school experience. Hence their pedagogical theories cannot function as a rational authority for the regulation and promotion of those social processes we call education. Their doctrines may have been the very opposite of the views and customs prevalent at the time, and they may rise far above the current level of esthetic and moral sensibility. But they are incapable of bridging the gulf between ends and means. The ends are without exception high and ultimate, but whether the proposed means are suitable for their realization can only be ascertained by a scientific examination, practical success being the final criterion. Yet these pedagogical theories are so constructed as to put them beyond the range of verification. However they may differ in content, presentation and systematic rigor, they rest alike on two fundamental constants that defy empirical examination and correction. These are the aim and the object of education. The views of the object of education, the child, are uncontrollably influenced by unconscious drives while the aim of education is treated as given.

The pedagogues will accept nothing less than the highest ideal—moral, social, religious, or intellectual—as the aim of education. It is beyond question, it exists for them prior to and independent of experience. If a more systematic mind among them felt obliged to arrive at it by rational means, his argument would be no more than an exercise in deception because he knows in advance what the result must be. The aim of education is well established before his thinking begins and he proceeds without risking unpleasant surprises. But where did he get this absolutely certain aim? Usually from his teachers and contemporaries, or, in more complicated cases, from within himself. He then experienced it as an intuited certainty that he must honor like the starry heavens above. The knowledge of the stars I leave to the judgment of the epistemologist; but of the moral law within I know that it is inextricably interwoven with the unconscious, and with all the evil, alien and uncontrollable forces within me. True, it points the way with a commanding voice and staunchly proclaims it to be the right one. Yet by obeying that law, I make myself the slave of a power of which I know neither the origins nor destination. I obey it willingly, and that establishes my guilt, not my merit. I experience this unknown power as a compelling norm and I believe in my experience, though I may regret that I cannot know that power. I discover with pleasure, and perhaps uneasiness, too, that my ideal of man is in essence apparently the same as that of Pestalozzi, Herbart and the rest. We all agree, we are in perfect harmony with regard to the aim of mankind. I, however, raise the question: who can prove that this is also the aim of education? The pedagogues simply assert the identity of the two, which is their noble error. In view of the utmost importance they attribute to education, how could its aim be other than the highest and all-inclusive? They do not understand that there can be any question here at all. What a St. Vitus's dance is this history of educational ideas! Were the universal human aim also the aim of education, education would be a matter of the greatest importance. But merely because educational theory prescribes, haughtily and nonchalantly, the highest tasks to educational practice does not exempt us from inquiring whether it is right in doing so.

I do not reproach the educators for having great and lofty

aims, but for charging education with their realization without asking themselves some simple questions. Is the eternal human ideal attainable? Can it be attained through education? In particular, can it be attained through the methods the educators have devised? These questions will be pursued later in a broader context. I state them here really to express distrust of all the theories about educational method that have been transmitted. A satirical history of educational thought could be written to amplify the harsh dissonances that exist between the eternal aims and the theories of even the most venerable educators. Here I merely point out a few data and will be content if the reader is stimulated, by his disbelief and opposition, to question and examine.

All educational measures for changing the child and its intuitively and naively interpreted psychic structure in accordance with that high aim are suspiciously simple and banal. None of them is new, and perhaps it is impossible to think up any new educational method. The great educators certainly did not succeed. They have run the gamut from love to harsh discipline, from verbal instruction to teaching by personal example. They have recommended that teachers play an active part, and that they practice patient restraint. They have demanded free expression for the child's impulses, and their repression. This whole scale has been tried ever since parents and teachers existed, and millions of children have been exposed to every imaginable combination of means and methods. And the result? Humanity as it is today, and always was. The distance between empirical man and ideal man remains essentially unchanged; it certainly has not been shortened in the course of millennia. We must not mistake civilization for moral progress. The varieties of cultural forms in which the unchanging psychic structure of man has expressed itself do not indicate higher or lower value levels. We conclude, therefore, that the trite and well-worn means of education do not possess the magic power of realizing human ideals that pedagogical systems ascribe to them.

Their defenders will rise and accuse us of exaggeration. They may admit the failure to attain ideals, but they will insist that educational theory be given due credit for achieving more modest aims, which may at least be stepping-stones to the ideal, such as the broadening of students' interests, the development of personality, or the teaching of spiritual values. But this objection does not invalidate my basic criticism. Educational theory is so constructed as to make it incapable of providing objective criteria by which the alleged effectiveness of *any* educational measure can be determined. The scientific attitude is replaced by self-confidence and intuitive judgment. The emotional power with which the great pedagogues appeal to us on behalf of their methods may help bring about the predicted success, and the independent value of a method becomes impossible to ascertain. Specific measures are credited with success, with never a thought for the unknown and uncontrolled factors present in actual educational situations.

Yet these and similar arguments already presented may still leave the reader unconvinced. He finds it hard to believe that a discovery should be made in this book that has eluded the remarkable minds who created the theory and philosophy of education. How is it possible, he modestly asks, that no one during the last two thousand years should have noticed that pedagogy is a castle built in the air? It seems to him that if this author is right, we are about to be ushered into a new epoch of education. But he remains incredulous.

Well, many a superstition has held firm for centuries only to be exposed one day, and those who accepted it were no more stupid or less remarkable than those who destroyed it. Nor is it so strange for an author to assert that he is ushering in a new epoch and to find a few believers. It has happened that such assertions turned out to be right. However, I need not stake my position on the slippery ground of this kind of argument. I affirm that the theory of education I have now defamed long enough was not and is not worthless. Its past and present dominion should not astonish in the least. It fulfills a certain function and is able to do so by virtue of the very attributes I have been criticizing. The unscientific character of pedagogy results from a number of psychic and social conditions and that in turn fits it to be an instrument of certain psychic and social forces in our society. To understand and describe this relationship is the job of an empirical science. I have here not been concerned with reporting the results of such an inquiry objectively. Rather I have valued and presented them from a certain point of view. The valuation I have chosen may be opposed by a contrary one. That will depend on whether the forces that demand an unscientific pedagogy are accepted as inevitable and affirmed as desirable. What these forces are will be the subject of the following chapters, and the function of educational theory will be better understood when we have grasped the nature and function of educational practice. The reader is of course free to accept the high value put upon educational theory by every teachers' college and to condemn my censure of it. But if he does, he should realize that he has thereby decided, possibly against his knowledge or will, in favor of one of the parties now engaged in world-wide social struggles. Perhaps I should have kept all these value questions from interfering with my account and limited myself to presenting calmly and objectively the relations that exist between education, the human psyche and society. But I doubt that, because those readers whose values differ from mine lack the necessary faith in science, and I would have bored the others who are on my side in the present struggle.

II

The Preconditions and Function of Education

Realizing that the philosophy of education is incapable of setting any limits to the practice of education because of its presumption of removing all criteria to the infinite, we are freed from the demands philosophy imposes upon practice and may therefore turn to education as it really is. We will attempt to ascertain its preconditions and function in society in the hope that we may perceive where its present limits lie. Only after such an examination is it possible to proceed to the discussion of whether the currently prevailing limits must also be accepted as necessary.

The first condition is provided by the natural fact of ontogenesis. Were children born physically, intellectually, and socially mature, there would be no education. Development would be assured by genetic mechanisms or determined by congenital processes. Since this is not the case and childhood exists as ontogenetic postnatal development, education becomes an inescapable social fact. The word social requires emphasis because a solitary childhood would not compel education. To conceive of such a condition within the human circle is impossible because man independent of social relations would be a phantom and no longer a human being. There are animal species and even genera in which childhood constitutes almost the entire life and lasts for months, whereas adulthood is limited, as with butterflies, to a few days or hours. Here childhood exists, but nothing resembling education because this kind of childhood is not passed in society. Childhood occurs as a result of inborn tendencies to react to the concrete conditions of life, accidental or general, which the organism encounters. Education exists only when, but always when, childhood is experienced in society. The biological fact and the social fact constitute its preconditions.

However the structure of human societies varies, the child claims a place in it from the moment of its birth. It requires a certain amount of social labor; certain institutions exist solely to promote child development; and certain attitudes, views, and behavioral patterns indicate that the social structure takes this into account and reacts to it. I suggest that we call the sum total of these social reactions education.

This definition enlarges the concept of education beyond its customary scope. And this is to be expected, for once education is regarded as a social process and not, as in pedagogy, as a system of norms and instructions, the number of relevant phenomena increases. An extreme example may help clarify the difference between pedagogy and our view, which we may call the scientific view. Pedagogy would not consider the differences in children's dress and fashions observed in different periods, classes, and nationalities as educational data, and it would not theorize about them. In the scientific view of education, however, these data acquire significance because they are reactions of society to the fact of childhood. Pedagogy fails to put any value on children's dress and fashions because it assumes that such social actions are irrelevant to the attainment of its aims. But relevance is a question for educational science to decide. It will determine whether such actions are "good" or "bad" education, relative to certain aims. Since, unlike pedagogy, it is value-free, the scientific view has no choice but to regard these and all other actions society specifically directs at children as education.

The conscious, deliberate effort pedagogy has in mind is education in the narrower sense and constitutes only a special case whose particular function has yet to be investigated. It is a late product of history and can hardly be understood unless we know the earlier function from which it became differentiated. Social structures have existed, and still exist, in which education in the narrower sense is unknown, but which all the same provide organized space for childhood and cultivate customs that later come to be called conscious education. Is there any difference between the severe glance at his son of an angry Kafir father and the exhorting, punitive glance of a Pestalozzi, just because one is lauded as means to an ideal end whereas the other originates wholly without reflection or aim in causes yet to be discovered?

We distrust pedagogy because we don't believe that the tasks it sets education represent its actual social function. We rather suspect that this function is meant to be concealed and to remain unknown. If deliberate education could at least be clearly delimited from the rest, we would have some reason for accepting the pedagogical definition of education, instead of enlarging it as we have done. But the one mingles with the other, and everything is in flux. We must therefore experiment with a looser, more comprehensive definition and see how far it takes us. Perhaps there is a single principle that uniformly determines and rules all the reactions of society to the fact of development, that is, its entire educational complex. Then our terminological extension would also mean a new understanding.

Such a possibility seems plausible from even a brief glance at the history of education and culture. In the second half of the eighteenth century, when the pedagogical revolution linked with the names of Rousseau and Pestalozzi occurred and the modern system of schooling was created, radical changes in children's literature and dress, in their rights and life style also appeared. A new conception of the child was expressed in literature and art, economics and politics, signifying a basic change of view on the part of the public. These subjects do not really belong to education in the narrow sense, but they seem to me mutually and functionally related even though their interdependence did not enter the consciousness of the age. Moreover, these particular changes in education coincided with others in culture and society and belong to the movements that coalesced in the Revolution of 1789, although their lasting effects began to take shape only later. They are finally related to the forces that form and transform society, to the system and direction of economic production. This by no means holds true only for the revolutionary epoch of the terminal phase of capitalism that began after 1789. Whenever and wherever transformations of education in the narrow sense are observed, corresponding changes take place also in the larger sense. Deliberate, conscious education is therefore not an isolated phenomenon but a symptom or consequence of an underlying change that I am tempted to call a change in societal reaction to the reality of development.

This kind of generalization, however, is foiled by a curious phenomenon, unnoticed by the theory of education, which suggests that the situation is considerably more complicated—namely, that there are constant factors in education. These constants are present in all the variable educational measures and institutions. They are as old as mankind itself and have remained unchanged through the whole course of history. Changes in the processes of economic production do not affect them, nor do religion, revolution, or cultural upheavals. And they are the same in different races, classes, and nations.

The constant factors are especially prominent in such educational behavior as occurs in pair relationships, that is, between a single educator—whether father, mother, or some other adult—and a single child. In every such relationship the possibility of conflict arises in which the educator's will does not agree with the will of the child. The adult then resorts to means for breaking the resisting will, for example by causing the youngster displeasure or pain —what we call punishment. Such punishment contains certain constants that may appear under all variable educational conditions and take the form of psychic reactions. These are generated by the affect that is aroused when one's will is thwarted, and they are expressed overtly unless inhibiting conditions obtain. Physical aggression follows the hostile affect unless fear of the enemy, or fear of other consequences of one's own aggression, inhibits it. In the isolated pair relationship all such inhibitions drop away because the adult does not fear the child. The affect runs its course even when it is not rational and no rational purpose is served. For all rational purposes are extinguished by the affect that substitutes its own, that of giving vent to the instinctive motor release of the emotion itself.

The conflicts and the absence of inhibiting forces are part of the fact of human development, just as the reaction to this is a fact of education. Conflicts between child and adult in the pair group are inevitable because being a child means living exclusively for one's pleasure while the group is not and cannot be so structured as to gratify every desire. The child is powerless for power rests ultimately upon physical force; and the adult need not fear the child, the most important and the oldest inhibitor of the spontaneous expression of the affects being thus eliminated. When ideological or moral scruples take the place of fear, the pair group is no longer whole but has been infiltrated by the effects higher ranking social groups exert upon it. But who can believe that such fear substitutes will work on a large scale and in the long run? Man is a slave of his psychic processes which after all make him what he is. The more his emotional life is inhibited by the groups that determine his physical as well as his mental survival and the more severe the restraints placed upon his original psyche by fear, ideology, morality, and religion, the more fully and deeply will he indulge his affects toward the child and know how to liberate himself from the fear substitutes too. Some philosophy is easily found by which to justify the emotional outburst—the term is used descriptively and not in judgment—as an infallible method for achieving the ultimate educational purpose it has already deduced. When all this is duly considered, no one can doubt that whenever men— not apes and not angels—act as members of a pair group, we will meet the eternal constant of the uninhibited outbreak of adult emotion.

The reader probably feels that I am railing against a state of things I wish did not exist. But this would be a misunderstanding I must correct. An affect is no more indecent than its expression is necessarily evil. What is true for punishments arising from aggressive states is equally true for the milder forms of education in the pair group that are generated by love. It, along with its uninhibited expression, is equally a constant reaction in this setting. Hence everything that has been said applies to love also, including the justification love seeks—and finds even today—in philosophy and pedagogy.

The educational reformers of today preach the gospel of love, which I like and gladly practice. But it would be an error to suppose that the gospel of love is more rational than the pedagogy of hatred. At any rate this has yet to be demonstrated. Nor is education through love anything new. Like its opposite, it is inevitably a constant and originates in psychic strata no less deep. It exists because of the fact of human development: children are loved for no other reason than that they are children. Toward this kind of love the inhibitions are less severe than toward the love of fellow adults: the one is allowed to flow more freely, the other is kept within narrowest bounds.

In our society, however—and this is a paradox—the love reaction is more inhibited than in others. American Indians, for example, shy away from inflicting severe punishment on their children. In extreme cases they scratch the hand of a sleeping child and in the morning show him the mark Manitou made. We run teachers out of town because they do not know how to maintain sufficient discipline, and never mind by what means. We are afraid of uninhibited love, far more than of uninhibited hatred, and rightly so. Hatred injures but a single human life, but uninhibited love threatens the established order and the structure of all lives, namely, capital and its power, as the science of the great Marx teaches.

The last sentence I would better not have written. It is not indispensable in this context and must come as a blow to quite a few readers. The wall with which philosophy, ethics, and other so-called knowledge have surrounded them since high school will now close even tighter and let pass still less of what I have yet to say. But if that remark was a didactic gaucherie, it will at least earn me the gratitude of the pedagogues. For their wisdom would be pretty nearly at an end if all my readers readily and faithfully drew the practical conclusion from the truth about the constants in individual psychology. After all, the overwhelming number of educational doctrines has been preoccupied with the pair group. It was the archetypal pedagogical situation for Locke, Rousseau, and Herbart and played a crucial role in the theories of Comenius and Pestalozzi. It remains the model for every theory that thinks of education in terms of the parental relationship, and exerts its influence also over the methods of formal instruction since the school is rarely viewed as a special social institution with consequences and functions of its own. The majority of educators rather looks upon the school as though it were a sum of pair groups and therefore misconstrues what goes on there. Their chief endeavors are misguided because they are directed to the constants in the psychic relation of adults to children, or what historically at least are unchanged types of human action. The history of this type of pedagogy is like a kaleidoscope in which the same components are used to form new figures, and sometimes quite attractive ones. But obviously no basic changes are possible. If the affective reactions we have described are malleable at all, other means than the study of pedagogical sermons will have to be found.

We must now analyze more closely the impression derived from the history of culture that individual psychic constants are subject to a limited variability. Some tendency toward the inhibition of aggression and toward the humanization of education in the pair group does seem to be at work. We have, of course, no reliable experience on this score because our knowledge of how people were brought up a hundred or three hundred years ago is inadequate. Almost all we know is how some people theorized about it, but the actual behavior of the masses, we are convinced, bore little resemblance to the ideals of the pedagogues. They are forever polemicizing and sermonizing. In the eighteenth century they preached to parents and tutors not to spoil and pamper children but to accustom them early to discipline. In the twentieth, they proclaim the rights of children and with equal ardor preach the gospel of love toward them. Those early evangelists addressed a type of parent who would be the delight of his modern counterpart, but at that time the tenderhearted parent was an object of pedagogical insult. Must we suppose that that type of parent no longer exists, or that everyone today rears his children baroque style? Obviously both types of behavior exist, as they always have, but their ideological justification changes from one epoch to another.

The statistics, too, may have changed. In the nineteenth century, for example, the number of adults with predominantly aggressive affects toward children may have increased, or it may have decreased. It all depends on whether the general humanization, which shows some progress, extended also to the pair group. Reverse changes are possible too, so that the love reaction becomes more inhibited. If one compares the children of the common people in Italy with those of the German middle class, one observes that they are bathed in a flood of parental love; and even though it is not infrequently interrupted by aggressive outbursts, it nevertheless flows more abundantly than in the German bourgeoisie.

Still, all such variations are relatively minor, they are difficult to prove and to state with any precision. The extremes of love and hate are probably rare, and some mixture of the two is the common occurrence. The same person is likely to be inconsistent and to behave differently in a sequence of situations. Actions that violate even a minimum of decorum may not be infrequent, without however being considered normal. Over longer stretches of history, there are indications of a certain humanization and moderation of aggressive behavior, along with a parallel tendency to inhibit the expression of love. But the evidence remains inconclusive, for the phenomena of cultural history are the result of an unknown mixture of individual and collective processes.

For a particular study of the collective processes, the life of primitive peoples and its social organization into age groups provide suitable objects. There the child grows up with the mother or the women of the tribe and is the recipient of uninhibited love. This, of course, does not preclude occasional experiences when his desires are denied or come into conflict with the aggressive affects of the adults. But these are rare and a very tender love of the mother for the child prevails. Restraints of shame and disgust or incest prohibitions scarcely interfere with their relationship. Even weaning, which seems to us a natural and unavoidable measure, is not practiced. The child remains at the breast until the next infant is born and then shares the pleasure until he voluntarily refuses it.

This paradisiac idyl of mother and child comes to a sudden end when preparations for joining the adult male society traditionally begin, somewhere between ages seven and thirteen. Then the boys are taken from the mothers, occasionally by force, and subjected to the wholly different treatment of the rites of initiation. Their duration, form, and content vary considerably even among neighboring and related tribes, but in every case the boys are removed from the mothers and segregated in the men's house, or in a special house for circumcision, in a sacred grove or magic wood. Here they are prepared for the main rite by fasting, bodily torture, and instruction. The rite consists essentially of solemn acts in which the fathers symbolically kill their sons and reawaken them to a new life, the life of men. They receive the tribal insignia, are circumcised and tattooed, have their teeth, lips, or ears mutilated and acquire a new name. They thereby assume their rights as men, which means primarily the freedom of sexual intercourse within the limitations fixed by the society.

Cruelty accompanies every rite and it frequently rises to the most exquisite torments. Ploss describes this endearing episode in the initiation of the Kafirs. The fourteen-year-olds are lined up, each holding a pair of sandals. Their elders, armed with long switches, stand or dance in front of them. "Are you going to guard the chief?" the dancers ask one of the boys. As he answers "yes," blows rain down upon him leaving bloody stripes across his back while he vainly tries to shield himself with the sandals. He leaps about grimacing but is not allowed to withdraw. To the next question, "Are you going to tend the cattle?" he again answers "yes," and again the blows descend upon him. If the boy passes this test, he feels himself a man and is accepted as one. If he fails, no Kafir maiden will ever love him.

In Australia the knocking out of teeth climaxes the ceremonies. The youths are brought by their fathers into the festive circle, and first the torments to which they must submit are described to them in the Kebarrah song. Then preparations for knocking out a front tooth begin. A rod of hardwood is inserted in a hole through a tree trunk. The end of the rod is placed against the tooth, and while one man holds the youth's head in position, another shoves it forward. This usually results in the tooth and part of the gum being torn out. Some of the bystanders threaten the boy with instant death should he express pain, while others cut long stripes across his back and shoulders with sharp stones. If the victim utters any complaint, the performers of the ceremony cry out that he is unworthy to enter the ranks of men. But if he endures without sign of distress, he is received into the rank of hunter and warrior. He is surrounded and presented with the mundi, a small piece of bright crystal kept hidden by the women of the tribe. Finally both the men and women welcome the initiated, who is equipped with shield and weapons.

Such rites are not the exotic result of the sadistic aberration of various peoples, but a general educational institution of typical and recurrent characteristics, which suggests that they are a necessary part of a certain social structure organized according to age groups. This structure may well represent, as sociologists believe, a general transitional phase in human development. It could be one of the oldest, if not the oldest, social structure we are able fully to reconstruct from its still extant remains. The rites from which our examples were taken are highly typical. We note especially that they constitute the oldest type of organized collective action of adults toward childhood. Whereas the child's early education by the mother lacks organization and "inventions" of any kind and consists of natural responses that are intelligible in terms of individual psychology, the aggressive orgy of the fathers represents an action of a quite different kind. The first is education in the pair group, the second is collective education in a majority group, organized in and by society. The aggression orgy is the beginning of organized education. Its organizational achievement lies in dissociating aggressive behavior from the pair group and gathering it, altered and intensified, into a new group that brings it to bear exclusively on children. When we compare today's conditions with that primitive state, we may claim the existence of a humanizing trend more justly than in a comparison between a few recent centuries. Still, the humanization of the means has been accompanied by an extension of their duration. Primitive peoples exposed boys to their very drastic educational measures for only a few weeks or months, while we with our admittedly far more humane means take from fourteen to twenty years. But lest we boast about how far we have come, let us remember that until recently fairly unhumanized initiation rites were faithfully preserved in the dubbing of a knight, in deposition, confirmation, and reception into the journeymen's associations of the guilds.

The meaning of the initiation rite cannot be understood in terms of individual psychic behavior. The performing fathers themselves do not understand it. They rationalize the rite by imputing to it purposes they can grasp and perceive it as a test of perseverance, courage, and endurance which effects a lasting imprint of the laws of the tribe and its gods. Their belief is exactly like that of our educationists: an established custom is justified by being designated the only valid means to a noble end. But the end has not produced the means, and the society and its individual members are unconscious of its *raison d'être*. Whatever part of it is psychically determined derives from the unconscious, which must be uncovered if the specific determinants are to be identified. The unconscious imperative commands the killing of the boys, yet the assembled fathers do not obey it. We do not know for certain why this is so and what prevents them. It could be their fear of the women, who are excluded from the rite, kept away by force and frightening noises. At any rate, the boys are not killed, at least not all of them, and we take comfort in the negative teleology that, after all, mankind would long ago have become extinct had not some cruel god prevented this solution which might have been equally fortunate for all concerned. The fathers do not really know that they wish to kill the boys, but all the same the initiation rite is a grand symbolic act of death and rebirth.

What is the motive for this urge to kill that is powerful enough to set in motion enormous social energies and to assert itself despite countless disguises and moderations? The fathers are in fact threatening the future male adult with what will happen to him in earnest—without any disguise, moderation, or symbolism—if he should murder his father and sleep with his mother. The gravity of incest and parricide is indelibly impressed upon the young generation by this prophylactic retaliatory act, as well as on the adults also, who, it seems, remain exposed to the temptation of these crimes and who doubtless experienced it in their own youth. Hence self-punishment has a part in the motivation of this primitive social act of education. It springs from the sense of guilt mankind contracted when it founded the first cultural society and totemistic order upon a parricide that occurred in the aboriginal horde. The initiation rite serves to prevent a repetition of that original crime, to atone for one's own lingering temptation and to establish and act out the sense of guilt. This is what the scientific mythos of the great Freud teaches.

This last statement was, once again, superfluous and prejudicial. Of course the reader will have noticed for some time that the train of thought in this book is influenced by Freud, a fact which presumably does not enhance his confidence in the author and his views. Still, the reader could, to this point at least, hope to meet at some appropriate place with that emphatic partial disclaimer already so dear and familiar to him from the current scientific literature, to wit: while we agree with this or that idea of Freud's, we cannot share his reckless exaggerations, although otherwise he is not wholly without merit. Perhaps the reader would like even more such a qualification as: the most vehement protest against the excesses of psychoanalysis notwithstanding. But now he is disappointed, for he here finds Freud recognized without qualification and his work serving as the foundation for the science of education. This may irritate those who agreed with the earlier parallel statement about Marx and correctly interpreted it to be the author's own view; which in turn may have displeased others who are partial to Freud. The way out of this dilemma is to construct a bridge anchored in both pillars, from which a broad view of the extensive educational landscape may be obtained. Such a construction has been in the minds of educational theory builders since Herbart, who attempted to erect a general theory of education on the dual support of ethics and psychology. Unhappily, these proved to be insecure. The unreliability of ethics is too obvious to require explanation. As to psychology, what was it before Freud except a superficial, ostensibly precise investigation of sense perception, association and thinking? And what is it today, apart from Freud's work, other than undisciplined speculation and the vain projection of hypersensitive and introspective bookish types whose ideas are both guided by and deflected from the unconscious? Only when this kind of psychology is replaced by the teaching of Freud, who puts development, drives, and character into the center of concern, can the science of education be provided with a foundation. This foundation will be sufficiently broad and solid to support the weight and height of any future structure so long as instead of ethics, political sociology (*Sozialwissenschaft*) in its most solid—Marxist—form supplements the depth and vitality of Freudian psychology. The motives for choosing these two scholars as patron saints of the new science of education will soon be explained. For the present we return from this digression to initiation rites and infanticide.

Infanticide as a social practice also exists apart from initiation rites, a fact repugnant and incredible to our century. Yet a substantial volume could be filled with accounts of customs that directly intended child murder and were part of the social organization and its educational institutions. I am not referring to brutal and sadistic individual acts that are punishable as crimes, though whole armies of children have been their victims in the course of centuries. I rather have in mind deeds like that of Father Abraham, who was prepared to sacrifice his son, whether from fear or love is always difficult to decide with such god-fearing people. He still enjoys the sanction of mankind, which now as then has no scruple in consecrating or sacrificing the life of a child to some higher purpose. It is a matter of taste whether the purpose is religious awe or political intent as in Herod, immortalized in countless paintings, or the extortionist tactics of Jehovah on behalf of the Israelites, delivered, with utter futility, from Egyptian bondage. In all these cases, the deed is not considered a crime, which shows that mankind is willing under certain conditions to remove infanticide from the realm of purely individual acts. Under Roman law children were subject to unrestricted paternal power. Our civilization, while it moralizes and sermonizes about it, permits hecatombs of children which, though unintentional, are nevertheless accepted as consequences of other social institutions such as war and death in factories. All these facts prove that now as always the killing of children is socially permitted and that this phenomenon is supported or produced by a murderous tendency that resides in the unconscious of the individual and his society—unless, of course, we hold God responsible for this and earlier worlds.

We are not inclined to derive and explain this whole variety solely from male guilt feelings, a term into which we compress the complicated body of Freud's assumptions. We would prefer to assume the existence of a general urge or behavioral pattern typical of the male psyche for which father Kronos devouring his sons might supply the prototype. This seems a viable hypothesis as many other mammals react similarly to their litters. Though females, too, may occasionally exhibit this reaction, we designate it as male because it is more common in that sex. Wherever there are primitive beginnings toward the socialization of that hypothetical arch-reaction, it is certainly male groups who are its agents.

It makes sense to talk about an originally male reaction only if it can be contrasted with a female counterpart, and this is not difficult to identify. Its presence can be sensed throughout the actions within the pair group preceding the initiation rite, and it is defined more clearly by a study of the care of nursing infants. For example, the babe is kept warm with the help of baths and wraps, and it is carefully protected against light, noise, and other stimuli which did not reach its original habitat but to which birth suddenly exposed it. It lies and sleeps in the natural embryonic position in the moist warmth of a covered cradle or with the mother in her bed. During the day it may be strapped to her body and share its rhythmic movements, or it is gently rocked in a cradle, much as it was earlier suspended and undulating in the fluid medium of the uterus.

It all looks as though the mother strives to reverse the radical separation of birth by keeping the child physically close to her, to protect and love it with that tenderness which is impossible to define adequately and for which the foetal situation may be more than just a biological analogue. This care is the polar opposite of the male reaction which, when attenuated, is reduced to the impulse of keeping the child away from the mother's body. The actual care of infants is somewhat removed from the primitive form—in most ethnic groups the latter remains only as a point of departure and ideal norm—and female and male behavior may be assumed to blend in varying degrees.

The very first steps a child takes mark a turning point in female behavior, and this occurs, strangely enough, at about the time the birth of the second child approaches. Now the mother must learn to bear a measure of physical detachment. Her original reaction is transformed into love which always consists in the longing to bring the child back into physical closeness and intimacy with her. For she loves it like a part of her own body from which it has been separated only temporarily. Otherwise love would turn into the most intense pain of separation.

While both the male and female archetypal reactions are collective phenomena, they also belong to individual personality in its deepest and normally unconscious strata. From there they act, in the form of unconscious individual constants, upon emotions of the tender or aggressive type, which we earlier described as individual psychological constants but must now distinguish from these deeper, unconscious ones as conscious.

The female reaction, whether it is repressed or built into the character, tends to intensify the tender emotions and to moderate the aggressive ones, whereas the male reaction will inhibit tenderness and reinforce aggressiveness. Other more complicated developments are possible where the repressed reaction may intensify its opposite by way of compensation and leads to other paradoxical behavior that Freud has taught us to interpret as products of repression. Also, a female may harbor the male type of reaction, and vice versa, so that both types may be active in the same individual in manifold blends and balances. But whatever the complications, they do not affect our chief assertion about an adult's educative behavior, its general principles as well as concrete acts. This behavior is determined by individual-psychological constants, namely, by the individual's release of his affects and by the structure of the original reaction in his unconscious or his ego. The pure pair group offers the most favorable social condition in which these constants may receive full expression in every educational action.

It is, unfortunately, not my task in this book to write the psychology of education. Nor is my topic the dawn of the history of education, which probably coincides with its psychology. I must instead pursue the question for whose sake I have ventured so deep into the underbrush of wholly unexplored territories. We are discussing the function of education, and although the material adduced may be inadequate and the hypotheses insufficiently illuminating, a provisional statement must now be attempted. We observed how the first educational arrangements had their psychological origins in the love of women for their offspring and in the destructive urge and fear of retaliation of the men. These psychological motives are still active today, though modified and overlaid. We have grasped the psychological determinants of certain educational arrangements and defined the age-old reactions of individuals to the reality of development. The question we must now take up concerns the social consequences of these reactions or their function.

With regard to the female reaction, the answer is simple. It ensures the physical continuity of society, and this is accomplished when the female reaction succeeds in depriving the male of its most primitive, extreme consequences. The female reaction need not be anchored in a special institution of exclusively feminine character. It joins the economic interests of the men in complicated societal forms, and it is guaranteed by the bisexual psyche of man which permits female tendencies to coexist in the male. Without a goodly portion of female intelligence no male group endures. Perhaps its safest anchor is the men's fear of women and their dependence on them as love objects. The female reaction may derive from a primeval human order in which the mother kept a firm rein on the males, her sons, through physical force and incestuous indulgence. A distant echo of that order may be found in the Greek heroes who trembled before the Amazons; and in the nineteenth century a careful scholar thought he could still detect certain remnants of the ancient "mother right."[5] At any rate, it is cer-

[5] An allusion to J. J. Bachofen (1815–1887), Swiss historian of ancient culture, and to his work on *Mutterrecht* (1861).—*Tr.*

tain and sufficient for our present purpose that history records no educational institution that can be ascribed to the female reaction. Its unadulterated expression occurs in the pair group of mother and child.

The function of the male reaction is less simple to define. What I offer here are not so much facts gathered from the study of relevant books, but some impressions and ideas about these facts in the hope of stimulating further research. While these ideas may seem self-evident to many, they still need to be impressed upon the minds of pedagogues. To make the function of male education clear, I shall begin with a schematic construction. The earliest beginnings of education may be conceived as analogous to that of animals. It is wholly a female affair. The carefully protected offspring is kept in physical proximity to the mother, and it grows and develops physically and psychically by recapitulating the history of the species. In short, the child matures and education ensures the form, content, scope, and periods of this genetically determined maturation. Perhaps it also promotes and influences this biopsychic process, but we cannot be sure. For contrary to the popular view, learning to speak may be a genetically determined process. The objection that a child growing up in isolation does not learn to speak is like the argument that the embryo learns how to grow from its mother since if taken out of her body, it ceases to grow.

The objection does contain a grain of truth: the direction and content of hereditary development require certain safeguards and influences in order to become actualized. As regards the embryo, these are concentrated in the mother whereas the child encounters them in his environment, taking this concept in its most extended meaning. In the midst of his worldly environment the child matures as though in a second maternal body. We are as ignorant about how "the morning breeze in mother's hair" affects the growing foetus as we are about the influences which Sirius, the moon and sun, the earth's interior, or its distant regions may have upon the growing boy. We are accustomed to this ignorance, yet we should also get used to admitting it, especially when making assertions about cause-and-effect relationships between certain aspects of the environment and certain aspects of maturation. Of course speech is learned—this is the word we use in describing what may be an action of the environment—but when does this learning begin? Breathing, movements of the mouth, the glint of the eyes, facial mimicry, and bodily pantomime are all maturational; but what in the environment promoted these activities and what obstructed them, we do not know. The rhythmic babble that already sounds like papa and mama is still maturation. We do not know exactly when and where it passes into learning.

Learning undoubtedly begins with vocabulary and grammar—and even then some doubts remain, inspired by the fact that infants almost to the age of two have everywhere a common grammar of their own. But who is to say which part of the milieu is indifferent and which indispensable to achieving equal learning success? Language, by the way, is not the most perfect example because it is in part an intellectual process, and how much of that occurred in our hypothetical primeval society is debatable. Anyhow, the child grows up and comes to be like others of his group by living among them; and having completed the great recapitulation, he is mature, a member of his society. He is not instructed in history because primitive society has as yet no history and no memory of ancestors. But it may have tools created by them and still currently in use, tools resembling a wooden extension of the arm or a convenient reserve belly for storage fashioned out of clay. If so, the final phase of maturation will be devoted to the young's acquiring these last inventions of organic life on earth, just as the first phase was reserved for acquiring life's most ancient solution to the social problem—how two individual cells, instead of devouring each other, may live together for mutual benefit and security.

This grandiose organic recapitulation presents the curious biologists, and the pedagogue no less, with a painful enigma. Whatever the causes and method of this gigantic compulsion, its result is ideally perfect. In nine months the embryo, which is the pupil of this instruction, learns the immense and undoubtedly tedious material accumulated over millennia with such perfection that he knows it in his sleep. Thanks to Freud, we know at least one important fact about the method of recapitulation, this course in higher education, as it were, that ends with the painful final examination of birth when the foetus's maturity is publicly certified. This method is the child's identification with his milieu, or what used to be called imitation as long as people still refused to acknowledge the existence of deep unconscious processes. The child identifies himself with the mother and with all living things in his environment in so far as he loves them. The emergence of such identifying love is ensured by the mother, who educates through lavishing love upon the child. This promotional method never fails with the nursing infant and, having once got through to him, maintains its hold upon the child. Thus, organic recapitulation, supplemented and extended through libidinous identification, turns the egg cell in a period of nine months and a few childhood years into a citizen-member of an animal or primitive human group.

I expect some kindly pessimist will ask, then why have schools at all? Why not abolish them and replace them with that superb method of organic recapitulation and libidinous identification? But that, my dear reader, is being too much of an optimist. Hold on to your pessimism instead, and try to understand that this has unfortunately become impossible ever since the occurrence of that ghastly event in human history that you had better read about in Freud's *Totem and Taboo.* You may find the story incredible. I do not and I am convinced that because of that event human society has suffered the kind of experience which, alas, makes it necessary to institute formal schooling and artificial methods in lieu of those natural ways. If, however, it were possible to make a less wretched job of education than we find in our kindergartens, I would turn optimist.

The "natural method" presupposes, first, learning material of a kind that can be acquired by identification. This is possible with attitudes, but not with contents of consciousness. Knowledge consisting of remembrances or concepts possessed by other persons cannot be acquired by libidinous identification. The latter follows upon perceptions; it assimilates and retains what is audible and visible, such as words and actions, but not the knowledge they symbolize. Unless knowledge is to die out with the generation that possesses it, it must be transmitted through instruction and acquired by a specific type of work, namely, learning.

We must not assume that animal or primeval human society possessed such knowledge. But in age-group societies, it already exists in the form of a collective institution. The boys from the back country of Liberia, for example, are abducted by force to the magic wood, the Grigi bush, where they live in seclusion for several months and receive collective instruction in dance, weaponry, law, and sexual mores. This instruction alternates agreeably with tattooing, circumcision, and other painful rites. In this magic wood the incipient school lies concealed. The difference between it and our contemporary, involved educational institutions may be considerable and impressive. But the principle, the organized transmission of a certain body of knowledge required by society, is the same. Also, some of the ancient sadism and of the orgy of aggression in whose shadow the school was first invented remains and transfigures it still today. Sometimes the light of that distant glory flares brightly, sometimes it glimmers faintly. At least that is the hymnic way educational methodologists may describe it. I, for my part, see no light at all, only darkness, though perhaps this is because I see only my own pessimism. Even so, we must not be unfair in our judgment of the school. It does not have an easy time of it. It is compelled to act counter to the children's inherited urges and against their spontaneous desires and interests. Whether methods are brutal or humane, it is forever in opposition to the powers of nature. To the child it represents the harshness and complexity of the social reality with which mankind has been saddled ever since the Fall, whether it occurred in paradise or in the primal horde. The school occupies the place of the angels who stand watch before the locked gate of the paradise of the original lost state in order to prevent old Adam from ever returning. Instead man is forced to create a substitute paradise of his own by sweat, renunciation and the sense of guilt. His success to date has been inadequate, but that is not the angels' fault.

The second requirement for the "natural method" of learning is less easy to define. The growing child must not only finish the course in recapitulation, he must at the same time achieve a psychic state in which he does not imperil his society nor feel himself imperiled as a member of it. The natural method, so perfect otherwise, has one grave defect: it is extremely conservative and not receptive to curricular innovations. The salmons' curriculum, for example, still includes the geography of millennia ago. They swim upstream for miles to spawn in places which in past geological periods were conveniently located near the mouth of the river. To salmons our universities must seem possessed by bolshevist radicalism, even though we do not dare abolish the Latin entrance requirement two hundred years after Thomasius[6] ventured to lecture in German. It is the last few millennia that have given education its hard and bitter nut to crack. The revolutions that occurred during that time have initiated new ways for the development of psychic urges that the curriculum of natural recapitulation completely ignores. Society is understandably proud of the innovations bequeathed by those revolutions, and it insists that everyone become familiar with them before certifying him as adult. All the same, the human species has not been exactly ingenious in finding new methods of coping with those innovations. It had an idea only once at the very beginning and has held on to it ever since: to extend and elaborate the original male reaction into an auxiliary supplementary institution. Such elaboration has become the real function of the male reaction.

To make this clear, we continue with our previous construction. It was assumed that the development of the child and especially the boy is marked by three turning points in relation to his mother. Birth turns him out into the world, but he remains physically in close contact with

[6] Christian Thomasius (1655–1728), professor of law at the Universities of Leipzig and Halle and a precursor of the Enlightenment, began lecturing in German around 1688.—*Tr.*

her. Next, as he begins to walk, he moves away from her body though it remains the object of his desires for rest and peace. He returns to it when he has had enough of his playmates, of the world and its disappointments. Now her body is no longer the only, but it remains the ultimate, object of his aspirations. Finally when he is sexually mature, he turns to her once more, not to seek rest but pleasure. She is then for him no longer mother but a woman like any other, the possessor of a pleasure-giving organ.

One consequence of those ancient revolutions that separate the primeval horde from human, though still primitive, society was to prohibit this last return. Adulthood was not to be a turning back, it was to complete the antithesis initiated by the second turning point and to consist in the eternal turning away from the mother. All other women may belong to the son, he may fight for them and have his choice as they have theirs. His mother is *hors de concours*. He and she have been irrevocably separated by the incest barrier. The prohibition originated somewhere, sometime within the primal horde, and is obscurely related to the other event of parricide. We know nothing about it and are thankful we are not ethnologists who have to unravel the tangled problems which the chronology of those distant revolutions pose and which have constituted mankind as it is. Suffice it to say that one of the innumerable consequences of the incest prohibition is education in accordance with the original male reaction. This is no cause for wonder because there is not a feature of post-incestual society that does not exhibit the aftereffects of those earlier events. Remote as they are in time, they remain timely and alive today.

To prevent incest the men took the boys away from the mothers; and to prevent murder they subjected them to the initiation rite. Through acquisition of the fear of incest and the sense of guilt, society and the individual psyche were enriched—and burdened—with elements to which organic recapitulation had no access. They were something new, something superorganic and remain so possibly even today, after having been repeated by a hundred thousand generations. With all respect for the conservative force in life, I am not inclined to credit it with the power to resist the obtrusive compulsion to adapt which this long chain of repetition represents; and I am willing to assume that society wanted these innovations—a most unpalatable subject—programmed into the organic curriculum. With their power to transform mankind and to form societies, these innovations, the fear of incest and the sense of guilt, rank indeed as inventions of absolute originality. We are used to them and take them for granted, at least as long as they do not occupy our minds or enter our own experience. We should, however, realize that nothing analogous exists in the whole organic and psychic realm. They are true super-achievements by which the biopsychic sphere transcends itself and which Freud conceives as the super-ego constructed over and above the id and the ego. Fear of incest and sense of guilt rank among the great original innovations, along with the processes by which life first differentiated and developed out of the inorganic. Tools, language, thought, and society are inventions of the greatest importance, but they do not present anything principally new when compared with those biopsychic revolutions.

One might be tempted to conclude from this that man's becoming socialized is accordingly of incomparable importance in the history of life on earth and that such a valuation is hard to reconcile with a pessimistic world view. But the thesis about man's development refers to certain facts and has little to do with a view of the world. That question arises only in connection with our judgment of the future. Regarding that, the pessimist will be disinclined to overestimate the chances for a favorable development. He finds that human nature on the whole has successfully resisted those innovations, and it is only through appropriate social institutions that a certain equilibrium may be maintained between the demands of the super ego and the age-old expression of primitive urges. Average man does not measure up to the demands and those who are sick or criminal fall far below them. Moreover, social institutions themselves do not enjoy the kind of stability that could instill confidence in the future. It is not impossible that sooner or later mankind may founder on its conflicts, and that would not greatly matter. Yet a few scant facts do exist to support a brighter prognosis. As I intend to explore this possibility in another work, I now return to the limits inherent in the power of libidinous identification from which this discussion started.

Those limits resulted from the fact that identification, being contingent upon perception, is only capable of repeating the behavior of the adults in the milieu. It is unable to introduce any innovation that would contradict organic recapitulation, or even promote or inhibit it. In the primitive state the mother is the object of identification and the fear of incest can therefore not be learned through her. The mother's mate, who is the male—if inferior—object of identification, also serves to arouse the prohibited incestuous desire. The fact that the father's attitude toward his own mother exhibits the required restraint can at best teach children incest fear of the grandmother, but not of their own mother. To attain this decisive aim, it is necessary to break up the mother-child group and transfer the child, before the advent of puberty, to a different milieu where the direction of the libidinous identification is changed. There the initiation rite enforces renunciation of the natural gratification of urges by absolute denial, fear and punishment. It reconstructs the affective powers and the ego by knowledge, myth and magic, and by newly discovered pleasures. All this the initiation rite achieves, having as its precondition the transformation of society into male alliances and age groups rooted in the original male reaction toward child development, the propensity for infanticide.

After all these detours and digressions, the function of the male mode of education should stand out clearly. It consists in the education of a psychic structure capable of preserving the attained social state, provided this structure contains an increment of principally new formations as compared with the original biopsychic one. The social function of male education is to gain and secure forever the cultural increment by which adult society preserves itself in the generation it rears. I have stressed repeatedly that the separation of the male from the female mode of education is just a scientific abstraction. In actuality they are combined and together fulfill the total function: the physical preservation of society, the safeguarding of organic recapitulation, and its correction and supplementation through the cultural increment by which the educative society and its psychic structure secure their continuity. I have dealt at length and in detail with the remote beginning of education because we know so little about the subject. As we approach the contemporary scene and our knowledge increases proportionately, I shall be considerably briefer. The dogma of the latest substitute for science will not detain me: masses of factual information only interfere with knowledge as cognitive vision. I am mindful of my original intention, which was not to write a psychology, sociology, or history of education, but a science of education. Although this science does not yet exist, I can at least project its outlines and prepare the ground by defining the limits of contemporary education and, indeed, of all education.

Some stages in the long history of education need to be briefly sketched. We may assume that male education very early penetrates the pair group. Without destroying it, the male intrudes into the female behavior pattern certain prohibitions, modifications, and reinterpretations that facilitate and secure the cultural increment. Examples of this shift in the onset of male education have already been provided. It tends to bring about an earlier separation of the child from his mother and to prevent her from tying him too closely to herself by uninhibited expressions of love. At the same time the father becomes a partner and one of the objects of libidinous identification; he insists on frequent and early denials of the recapitulative development of the child's urges, weakens them through fear and finally rechannels them by teaching the child to overcome the fear and create new forms of pleasure.

The success of these and similar measures has been astonishing; they have resulted in a greatly prolonged period of childhood. Rites of a few weeks' duration were eventually changed into a psychic development which in Europe today stretches over nearly ten years. Childhood now extends to about age fourteen and is followed by two years of puberty so that a European youth reaches maturity at sixteen, whereas his primitive ancestor got there between ten and thirteen at the end of the initiation rite. What is more, cultural evolution introduced into this process complications and differentiations of the greatest educational significance. Originally, physical and psychic development in beast and primitive man alike advanced equally along parallel lines, and maturity in both was reached simultaneously. This also conferred "social" and sexual maturity, and no one could prevent the young adult from behaving accordingly.

Culture has separated these developmental processes from each other so that they proceed along different paths and terminate at different times. Social maturity, for example, depends on cultural factors, such as class and income. A fifteen-year-old proletarian youth who earns his living in a factory is not legally of age and his coworkers and relatives may not treat him like a grownup. Yet he enjoys certain liberties, sex included, of which he avails himself according to his physical and psychic maturity, and public opinion sanctions this. His coeval in the classical gymnasium, by comparison, will indulge in those liberties in secret and with a sense of degradation as if he were committing a crime. Psychic maturity, too, depends more on cultural factors than on the physical state of sexual development. The psychological readiness to perform adult functions in love as well as in economic and cultural life may occur prematurely. In that case, a weak or not fully developed body will let that readiness atrophy into fantasies or become victimized by repression, and this ruin will be accelerated by the social forces represented in the youth's educative environment. Freud has shown that this is the normal case and occurs relatively early in childhood. On the other hand, psychic maturity may be delayed months and years beyond the advent of physical maturity. Then the discrepancy between physical urges and the resistance, ignorance and anxiety of the ego produces the emotional turbulence we call puberty. This state may continue far into the twenties, or it may subside early and yield to an inner adult peace which turbulent heads scorn as philistinism. Animals and primitive human society experience none of these difficulties.

Soon after the revolutions caused by fear of incest and sense of guilt, a development of singular significance for education occurred in the area of economics. Primitive economic life underwent radical changes, in the course of which social power, property and economic inequality originated. In some obscure way guilt and sexual possessiveness were transferred to economic activity and its objects. The new society, having first transformed sexual life and enriched the biopsyche with the increment of culture, began also to subject economic life to reform. Seemingly the most objective of all human affairs, it too was drawn into the libidinous sphere of influence where guilt is the operant power. The fearless scholar may discover that the ultimate causes of the flowering and decline of entire cultures are determined by the autonomous laws of economics. Yet in a still deeper sense the events of world history are a consequence of the sense of guilt that already penetrated economic life and society as a whole at the dawn of human history.

It is possible that some catastrophe like the ice age forced or promoted this whole process. Perhaps it was necessary and served some final purpose. Yet the social theory that rightfully calls itself socialism seeks to liquidate it. Of course no pessimist will be so immodest as to expect that he of all people will be granted the favor of witnessing the final end of so long and confused an epoch. Indeed, he will doubt whether there are signs that the beginning of a longer and happier epoch can reasonably be expected, and not merely longed and hoped for. If, like the author of this book, he has his moments of serenity, he will confess that his skepticism is not without a touch of ill will and *Schaden-freude* toward future generations. At any rate, since those early interactions of the sexual and the economic life, human society has ceased to be that simple structure in which the various human activities were clearly separable from each other. There is no economic trait that is not colored by sexuality, however refined and sublimated, just as every biopsychic impulse is constrained by concrete economic conditions.

At this point I should like to cite some other authors so as not to be solely responsible for views which many readers may not share with me. Unfortunately, none of the authors I have read is sufficiently clear and detailed or adequately in command of both fields to be able to describe the interactions between economic processes and biopsychic reactions. The shallow psychologizing of sociologists has long been recognized in all its tediousness. Neither human wishes nor ideas are the driving force of economic life. On the contrary, those wishes arise from economic life, and the ideas serve as justification of or as protest against it. The deeper psychic structure of man, however, remains unaffected by changes in the forms of production and their ideologies. Much of economic and social life may be interpreted as a transposition of the drives of a human soul. It seems as though the economic system were a kind of material embodiment and justification of the social unconscious, a kind of ideology of guilt. This sort of thinking can make Marxists awfully angry while the sympathies of the psychoanalysts are easily lost if one asserts that all the same Marx is right. Both Marx and Freud are right, though not the Marxists or the Freudians. One is reminded of the story about the zeppelin. The brave stalwarts who saw in

Freud's theories the confused and mediocre cogitations of a perverse Jewish mind thought they could destroy him by asking the question: Is the blimp a phallic symbol or an inventor's ingenious construction that serves a useful function? Nowadays any high-school student knows that a phallic symbol can indeed be a useful aircraft because the one designates a mechanism of the psychic inventive achievement and the other an evaluation of the technical achievement.

The solution to the psychic-economic dilemma is equally trite. An army, for example, is a structured mass "in which each individual is libidinously tied both to the leader and to the other individuals in the mass," to quote Freud's reprehensible "reactionary, bourgeois" sentence. But the army is *also* an instrument of the ruling class for the protection of its national monopoly of exploitation, its power, and profit. The first view looks at the army's psychic mechanisms, the second at its social function. In no sense, however, is the army a shield for Germany's highest national values, which claim is only maintained to guard against defeatism. Will my dear comrades understand that there is a capital difference here?

It is possible to concoct even more comic dilemmas. By way of mocking sexual enlightenment, childish minds of all ages ask which came first, the hen or the egg and, similarly, the biopsychic structure or the economy? To such inquirers I point out that they will take for an answer neither the hen nor the egg because they do not want to believe me at all. They really want to know something else —whether, for example, I am going to vote middle class or communist. To more mature adults one could perhaps explain that the egg was without doubt the beginning of everything; but if they mean the hen's egg, they would have to be told that the hen preceded the egg. Likewise, the biopsychic structure existed before the economy, which came about as a reaction of this structure to economic want. A given economic system may thereafter cause changes to occur in the biopsychic structure. As, however, these artless adult questioners are blockheads in all matters of human enlightenment, I would reply that this is a very difficult problem and I defer my answer until they have made a thorough study of biology, psychoanalysis, and sociology. I do not presume to give a neat statement of the sociological relationships involved in these problems, but continue along the zigzag course of this discussion, more curious and impatient than the reader to discover where in this thicket the markers indicating the limits of education may at last come into view.

I may astound everyone if I assert that there exist natural and unnatural economic systems and—an even triter observation—that animals generally resort to the natural type. They acquire food directly: they hunt and consume the booty in proportion to the individual's strength and participation in the activity. When, however, the work load for some is reduced while their share of consumption increases and when some surrender their share to others, not from love but because exploitation is socially sanctioned, a very different economic system has appeared that is alien to the biopsychic structure and forms a part of the cultural increment. The function of education is then to transmit it to offspring who would otherwise not assimilate the necessary behavior nor learn how this economic system is embodied in law, custom, and religion. No matter what the prevailing social structure, education must to a degree fulfill this special function because its general purpose is the preservation of society on the existing level of culture. But there

66

are two situations in which that special function becomes all important: first, when economic activity requires an extended period of preparation and training, and, second, when it is enforced by power.

The first situation is easily grasped with the help of a hypothetical case. Suppose men were to starve to death unless every adult was able to memorize the content of five thousand books. An intricate system of education would have to insure that every child begin this labor in his first year and conclude it by the time of his maturity. To perpetuate itself, such a society would likely have to kill off those who did not attain the annual quota of knowledge; and to end up with a sufficient number of survivors, every second of childhood would have to be controlled and the entire educational system subordinated to this overriding task. In this case, education would fulfill the function of transmitting the culture by concentrating upon one of its elements at the expense of all others. Though our bourgeois-capitalist society is a huge store of absurdities, this particular absurdity it does not harbor, either in a literal or a symbolic sense. One cannot complain that our process of economic production requires of its workers a long and intricate preparation. It has been and in large measure still is the case that the overwhelming number of specialized activities making up the total output can be performed by children between the ages of eight and twelve with little or no training. Children lack physical strength, experience, and endurance, but as they grow older, they acquire these naturally or under compulsion. A young person can be trained in a few weeks or at the most in one or two years; no kind of special training during childhood is necessary. Only a few occupations, those of rope dancers, piano virtuosi, and hereditary monarchs for example, require early training, and they are economically unimportant. One need only destroy the deep-rooted superstitious conviction that diplomats, politicians, and bureaucrats, the legal and the banking professions require an extended specialized education and years of training to realize that economic preparation is generally not a central function of our education. The economic system is not an element of the cultural increment which education has the function to transmit. Despite this, our education is geared to the economy from birth on. The reason is obvious: it is an illustration of the second situation mentioned above. Our education is ruled by power.

This fact complicates distressingly our simple formula for the function of education. Even more distressing, that situation is being obscured, and not least by the theory of education itself. How this all came about the reader can find out for himself by turning to the relevant literature. Here we are not concerned with the history of capitalist class society, but only with the simple and essential fact that in our society the economy satisfies not hunger, but the jaded appetites of a small minority, the ruling class. The ideal economic condition to which this society aspires is one in which the ruling class is freed from all physical labor and its economic activity is reduced to consumption and the management of production. This type of activity is artistic, playful, and free; in other words, truly human. What makes this refined and cultivated economic order vulnerable is that it does not please the majority, and why the latter has not simply liquidated the minority is hard to understand. It has certainly thought of doing so and on occasion attempted it. One reason for its failure is that the ruling class, not content to control the economy, occupies all the leading positions in order to secure its economic power. Another reason is the logic inherent in the system, called in this case the laws of capital. Among them is a factor that concerns the science of education more than the science of economics. The domination of the ruling class is disguised. Not only does the exploited majority depend in important ways on the interests of the ruling class and lose the thrust of its own power through the desertion of large groups, such power as it still retains the bourgeoisie knows how to divert from the real enemy by offering pseudo-enemies against which the majority may discharge its hostility and after a succession of futile revolts become resigned to its impotence.

Owing to the working-class movement and Marxism, this deception has not entirely succeeded. Also, the interests of the bourgeoisie are themselves subject to the laws of capitalism, which puts a limit to exploitation and admits a measure of social reform. Finally, in the past the bourgeoisie pursued revolutionary aims against the dominating feudal class, and in these efforts it required the help of the proletariat which has to be repaid, if grudgingly. Against all these adversaries the ruling class wields a highly respectable weapon, education, to which it imparts a certain bias in order thereby to protect its power. This particular purpose is not achieved if education serves merely to make the cultural increment secure in the younger generation. Fear of incest and sense of guilt with all their psychic and intellectual consequences, the whole panoply of European creativeness, ability, and knowledge, including mastery of the modern technology of production, by no means imply an affirmation of the bourgeois-capitalist order. The power of the bourgeoisie rests on force and coercion, and since it is sustained and perpetuated by these same means, it does not really require any education. This was the situation for a long time. Prior to Pestalozzi, whoever thought of educating the "poor?" But when its class rule is imperiled, the bourgeoisie introduces a bias into education in order to facilitate thereby the exercise of its power and to paralyze the countervailing forces that arise through the organization of the working masses. Education thus becomes an object of public interest.

A clever, class-conscious Machiavelli might, if he were so imprudent, express this bias in these terms: children must learn to love the bourgeoisie, and their love must be so deeply ingrained in them that a whole life of want and slavery cannot extinguish it. What in fact is forced exploitation must be made to appear to them as a voluntary and sacrificial offering of love. They have to produce surplus value, but they must do it gladly as if compelled by love, much as a lover waits upon his beloved or a religious believer upon his god. By Jove, citizen Machiavelli is a shrewd man. We therefore appoint him Minister of Education and authorize him to bring off this devilish feat. Fox that he is, he does not prepare himself for the job by studying experimental instructional methodology. He does not take a single course with Spranger.[7] He reads neither F. W. Foerster[8] nor Stern's[9] work on child psychology, though he has a

[7] Eduard Spranger (1882–1963), at the time professor of pedagogy and philosophy at the University of Berlin, author of *Psychologie des Jugendalters.*—Tr. [See the preface.]

[8] Friedrich Wilhelm Foerster (1869–1966), an educator whose academic career came to an end at the University of Munich in 1920 because of his outspoken antinationalist and antimilitarist views. For several decades, mostly spent in emigration, he continued to attract many readers by his writings which ranged widely over ethics, industrial society, politics, and the problems of education.—Tr.

[9] The reference could be to either of the following:
Erich Stern (1889–1959), psychologist, professor at the university of Giessen and director of the *Institut für Psychologie und Jugendkunde* in Mainz. Writings on psychiatry, psychology, and education. In 1933 emigrated to France.
William Stern (1871–1938), professor of psychology and director

diabolic way of praising both. Of psycho-analysis, however, he has a profound grasp. Before the privy councilors and his ministerial advisers he delivers this long programmatic speech (shortened transcript):

"To attain our goal, I propose the following organizational measures. You should understand that the crucial problem is the organization of education. This, I insist, we reserve as our exclusive sphere of influence while leaving curricular, instructional, and even pedagogical questions to the educators and ideologists. We may be so liberal as to admit Social Democrats among the latter, but solely for tactical reasons. A claim for their admission will be expressed, we let them fight for it a long time, and finally grant it in the form of a concession when a diversion of public attention is deemed necessary. Now our first organizational requirement is the segregation of middle-class from proletarian youth. I remind you that we are in secret executive session and that this statement is not to be quoted in the press. Nor is publicity necessary, for this middle-class youth comes from families who are quite safe from proletarian infiltration in the current generation. The number of these youths is small but everything depends on them. It is by no means necessary to bring them up in separate schools which would arouse undesirable attention. The financial and social status of their fathers already guarantees them an undisturbed education. They are destined to be the hereditary rulers of our society and economy, wielding power without external trappings, even anonymously. It will be good for them to experience the charm of this anonymity early and to test their capability for such a role

---

of the psychological laboratory at the university of Hamburg. Writings on psychology and education. In 1933 emigrated to the United States. —*Tr.*

during their school and university years. In appearance they will be the same as all other students but in reality they are the rulers even as they scribble on their slates. Incidentally, the slate should be abolished. We can never stage enough mini-revolutions of this sort. You will hear the country reverberate a whole decade over the important issue of whether first-graders should start with slate or paper.

"When I say that middle-class children should be segregated from the rest, I do not include among the latter the children of families whose future social class is uncertain. These will be brought up together with our hereditary rulers and owing to libidinous identification, as Bernfeld calls it, they will attach themselves to our princes of capital and become their lifelong vassals. Their loyalty is of course, as in the feudal vassals of old, a provisional one. They will earnestly strive to occupy the place of the prince, to conquer his land—I am speaking figuratively, of course—and to kill him. Yet though they are the personal enemies of all property owners—their salary is barely enough to live on— they will never attack the institution of property with which they are identified. A strong identification generates hopes that lifelong disappointments cannot dash. In short, I recommend the creation of a stratum of intellectuals recruited from the quasi-middle class and segregated educationally from the proletariat. Through the power of identification this stratum will be tied forever by its aspirations and its way of thinking to the propertied class.

"This psychological basis will bar the intellectuals from gaining insight into their own economic situation and let them struggle for individual opportunities of economic improvement—these chances are slim but exist in principle— in accordance with their ideal. It is the only way to create those paradoxical human types who fight for property without owning any: the solidity of our class rule gives them the chance to realize their ideal; in fact, the chance is as good as the actual realization. We shall not allow these young men to know the economic realities before the age of twenty or even twenty-five. Instead they shall have the pleasure of tasting the happiness wealth can bestow, and this will be indissolubly associated in their minds with youthful eroticism, freedom, and uproariousness. During those dangerous years when young rebels are apt to raise questions about social justice and right, it is important that our young men should remain ignorant of society as it really is. But if later on they should find out, they will no longer be able to eschew the advantages it offers them. You will see that because of the philosophy they have absorbed, they will unreservedly affirm our society. Students whose fathers will not or cannot provide them with a generous allowance will not be tolerated in the universities because such fellows are extremely subversive.

"I warn you, gentlemen, not to meddle with pedagogical questions. You are officials of the Ministry of Education and as such you are not to have any opinions or convictions, but to maintain strict neutrality in instructional matters. Occasions may of course arise when you will want to give a different impression. What these middle-class schools do with the young scholastically is a matter of complete indifference. Think this idea through! The only thing that matters is whom they admit and whether they give that quasi-bourgeois youth an opportunity to learn to appreciate the comforts and pleasures of a cultivated life. With that comes the knowledge that these comforts are secured, and made secure for them, too, solely by the continuity of our excellent system. Our model will be the English college though I would recommend a different name such as *Landesziehungsheim*[10] or 'school commune,' the latter in order to confound the revolutionary part of youth. Don't shake your heads. We cannot afford to be petty. I shall attempt to abolish instruction in these schools entirely though a transitional period will be necessary. During it, and with due regard to the principle that education must have relevance to youth, we shall fill adolescence, which is the idealistic period of life par excellence, with big words, such as fatherland, culture, nation, science, art, race, and—once more—culture. The teachers will be instructed to believe that these are the criteria of progress. They will demonstate that recent centuries represent a chain of fortunate developments interrupted by revolutions that were destructive of cultural values, whereas movements of national restoration augmented these values. Being the more cultivated, well-to-do, and happy, our class is the representative of the people, who are to be raised to this level. Until then we will always use the term 'people' rather than 'our class.' None of the teachers, I wager, will encounter any difficulties here. The classics and poets of the last century provide useful and relevant reading material. But please, no pedantry! We are not in the least interested in having these young people learn anything. *They* must not be old-fashioned, though it is to our advantage to have the socialist parties inclined that way. Our job is to impart to the young a firm ideology; and ideology is not learned, but grows spontaneously from the pleasures of a parasitic life. With the help of a few slogans

---

[10] A special type of country boarding schools, the first of which was founded by Hermann Lietz (1868–1919) in 1898. Lietz called these institutions *Heime*, or homes, rather than schools because they were intended to create a close familylike community of educators and pupils.—*Tr*.

we shall bestow on this spontaneous growth the authority of a cultural value. Furthermore, education must instill in our youth a sense of their own dignity. It must be convinced of its nobility, beauty, and cultural mission. Do not hesitate to borrow from Wyneken[11] for this purpose, it is perfectly safe. You will eliminate all possibility of danger by transferring their sense of dignity to their social class. Of course we shall always refer to the people and to German nationhood, not to the bourgeois class. True, the German people resists the concept of nation and this constitutes a great danger. We may, however, counter it by a relatively minor reform that requires no more than the courage to commit an utter stupidity.

"What we must do is to convert the unconscious anxiety of the Germans, which is deeply rooted in a sense of inferiority, into aggression. They must be made to believe in an immensely powerful, common enemy who threatens our —I mean the nation's—sacred values and who can be destroyed by a prodigious common effort. Care must be taken not to select a real enemy, the French for instance, because that would produce a realistic fear. Besides, if they were defeated, we would be back where we started. We must settle on something that really is nothing at all. That would offer the advantage of employing certain romantic traits that appeal to the Germans. How about a secret alliance of alien elements dedicated to the persecution of everything truly German? Large masses of people can be made to identify deeply with a leader and each other if they feel threatened by a common sinister danger. Do you begin at last to understand what I propose? Starting with the quasi-bourgeois chaps, we put our youth and then the entire pub-

[11] Gustav Wyneken (1875–1964), advocate of a special youth culture.—Tr. [For his relationship with Bernfeld see preface.]

lic in a state of panic fear: a sinister power threatens them and we come forward as their savior and leader. Read Professor Freud's *Group Psychology* and you will be convinced that my plan will succeed. I hope the socialists won't catch on; fortunately, they seem to take him for a bourgeois. In the situation I envisage, those individuals who are the epitome of the bourgeoisie will become the ideal of the young, and under its spell youth will form itself into a proud exclusive community we can lead where we wish. If only we had an enemy! He is hard to find because he must not really exist and yet be credible.

"I recommend we appoint the Jews the enemy. They pose no threat. They number only six hundred thousand (including wives, children, tuberculosis, and cancer) in a population of sixty million. That is the right proportion and in every other respect, too, the Jews are a handy people. They themselves will help us achieve our plan in one way or another. And if they should happen to get beaten up or killed, a sufficient number will survive elsewhere to keep the fear of them alive. Now, with the help of a carefully nurtured and dispensed anti-Semitism we sustain that proud middle-class youth in the high opinion of its own value, in its sense of national and racial aristocracy. Such value consciousness will in turn kindle identificatory aspirations among broad sections of the proletariat, and this is the attitude we count upon.

"Turning now to educational organizations for the proletariat, we adhere to the principle, which is in harmony with the interests of industry, that the place of proletarian youth is in the factory and in economic life generally. As to the proletarian children, it is in the rational interest of capital, if perhaps against the wishes of individual entrepreneurs, to exempt them from work for a time and collect them in schools. For our purpose the most propitious age at which to begin school is six. Psychologically speaking, the child is then in the midst of a significant catastrophe or has just passed through it. Under the stress of strong anxiety feelings, he has capitulated before the possessive power of the father and renounced possession of his beloved mother. Hence he is in search of new love objects and he will find these in the persons of his teachers, preferably unmarried women who are our agents. At the same time the child has gained a deep insight into his own inadequacy that makes him willing to submit to authority. Also, this tendency is fostered by a sense of guilt, by a willingness to undergo punishment, that formed in his ego during the early struggles and withdrawals. In the event that any rebelliousness should awaken in him, the authority of the school will deal it a searing defeat. We will take good care to make the school a national and state institution and succeed thereby in teaching the child to perceive state and nation as an enlarged family. This is, of course, basically false and only partially true even for our state. But it creates a psychological atmosphere favorable to the state's continuing existence and a shield against radical social revolution.

"The school, I say, is just like a family. There is the father with the handsome title of principal who commands and punishes, who is kind to those who behave themselves but remains above all remote and overpowering. There is the mother, the woman teacher, friendly, close, loving, yet moody, and in fear of the principal. She too can be won over, and more demonstratively so, by anyone who is a good boy. Finally, there are the child's schoolfellows, brothers and sisters, and equals all by law and custom. Still, free competition prevails and anyone who is able—in learning, cheating, flattery—or who is full of energy can get to the top

77

of the class and first place in the teacher's heart. The educational content and mission of this institution consists in making bookish knowledge supreme and placing its value beyond doubt.

"Proletarian schooling is crowned by the organization of adolescence, to which I have given especially careful thought. That period of life is rocked by a new wave of authority rejection and by the desire to subject life, one's own and that of the whole, to a sort of ethical revision. We must endeavor to preserve the fruits of childhood education from this peril, and to this end we abandon the young proletarians to their economic destiny. They will be urged by their parents to become financially independent and, unless we intervene, their life during apprenticeship and in the factory will resemble that of proletarian adults. Indeed, the burden of exploitation they bear will be heavier since one may expect the unions to defend their interests less vigorously. They will perceive—unconsciously, of course—the factory and all of economic life once again in the terms of affective family relationships, for which the school has prepared them. In other words, their aggressions and wooings will be directed at individual superiors or entrepreneurs. The socialist parties will have difficulty in making them see the bourgeois class behind these. Anyway, such enlightenment would not penetrate the deeper psychic layers. Since adolescence is a period of intense sexual urges, the young will be driven to sexualize their economic activity because this narrow factory-family leaves no room for sublimations. In their unconscious thought, the economic and the sexual sphere will become confused, with the result that the proprietor and entrepreneur, or his director or shop steward becomes a father to them. For the vast majority the main force of their aggression and rebellion has thereby been broken, no matter how noisy its expression. These urges are paralyzed by the memory of the infantile catastrophe that arose from an identical situation, and they are held in check by the same unconscious love for and identification with the father-entrepreneur. This identification will be reinforced by the adolescents' economic independence. If there remain some who look for an escape because they realize what keeps them in economic slavery, they will probably aspire to the life of segregated middle-class youth and seek an education, lured on by the school and public opinion as well as by the clever confusion between culture and education that even the workers' parties will find difficult to expose. The kind of education they seek will obviously be that upon which, so they believe, the value and power of bourgeois youth and society rest. They won't find it. . . ."

Minister of Education Machiavelli went on like this for a long time until the astonishment, surprise, and finally the rage of the privy councilors made him realize that what he was proposing already existed, only that he was presenting it in a subversive, cynical, untrue, and non-ideal fashion. No doubt this first administrative act of his was also his last. We allowed him to continue at such length because his speech is, I think, most instructive of what I called the social bias of education. However, he spoke of education mostly in the narrower sense and placed too much emphasis on the psychological point of view.

Social bias rarely creates an educational institution or organizational measure but colors them all. It supplies the required ideology and justification while suppressing other rival institutions, measures, and ideologies. Such bias is absolutely indispensable to class society and to every society that rests on power. I wish to reserve for the last chapter a more thorough discussion of how it relates to organized re-capitulation, libidinous identification, the cultural incre-ment, and the function and constants of education. But here we must already consider the fact that the cultural increment includes knowledge and forces that tend to op-pose the existing order, along with its economic system and the present distribution of power. The function of educa-tion should consist in transmitting to the younger genera-tion both the existing order and the forces that oppose it. However, social bias restricts this preservative function by the injection of certain values that cause the opposing elements to be debased and to become defunct, so that the young steeped in this bias help to fortify the position the ruling power occupies. Social bias necessarily depends on an authority that has the power to enforce it. In the final analysis this power rests nowadays with international in-dustry and finance.

In exposing the social bias we have not, however, reached the end of the complexities. This is regrettable for an author who must try to clarify the whole involved structure in a short space without becoming boring. The humane reader who has little interest in these theoretical endeavors and who rather wants to know what is to be done, will be thank-ful. Be that as it may, one thing is certain: education in our age is controlled and colored not by one bias but by two. These correspond to the two power groups whose unde-cided stubborn battle makes life on this unhappy planet so insecure, disagreeable, questionable, and dark. Perhaps life can be made bearable only by assigning as its meaning, such as it is, this gigantic and stupid battle. We no longer live in a time of stable bourgeois rule. That idyllic state may never have existed at all, though romantics and sentimentalists may be forgiven the illusion. Socialism has become a power center affecting, among other things, education. I am actually referring to the workers' movement that on the whole embodies socialism today, but I will continue to use the latter term. Socialism has neither vanquished nor replaced the capitalist class. Socialism has, however, limited the uses of its power, and forced it into indirect, devious channels and compromises. At the same time socialism has provoked capitalist countermeasures in the form of increasing self-protection, repression, and tendentiousness. What particular actions and reactions are taken depends on whether the relative strength of socialism is rising or declining. We are here concerned only to point out that, given two power centers of varying stability and influence, ideology and social bias are bound to attain exceptional importance for education.

Socialism would have been the victor by 1918, had it been able to take hold of the entire working class. Economists may examine what causes were responsible for obstructing the expansion. We are concerned with the psychic components of the situation and formulate them thus: the workers lacked insight into their exploited condition and could not conceive of a society differently structured. Or they lacked the necessary courage—it was sapped by bourgeois society that indoctrinated them with the pricelessness of its culture and the inviolability of private property, person, and law, now all questioned by socialism and threatened with revolution. Or again guilt and anxiety prevented the workers from carrying out the revolution, from murdering Father Wall Street and Mother Property and Capital. The ruling groups have many means of obscuring the true situation and maintaining a high level of anxiety, and of these ideology is the most efficacious. The Minister of Instruction will not be allowed to speak like citizen Machiavelli as long as the bourgeoisie may hope to disguise its organizational measures and conceal their intent. The actions by which it aims to weaken the opposition are always accompanied by some gesture or justification designed to recruit converts from the exploited in the depths of their ignorance and discouragement.

Socialism too requires an ideology for the same reason, but its ideology does not require mendacity. It is the intelligent and courageous statement of its means and ends. All it wants is the destruction of the ruling power in order to exercise its own. That is the banner with which it makes converts to its cause. For the imprisoned and suppressed, .liberation is a self-evident aim which requires no further justification. All they need is to recognize that their prison walls are not natural or inevitable and to acquire the courage to abandon their accustomed place. Through education socialism will transmit this insight and courage to the young, making them class-conscious and revolutionary so that they may accomplish the act of liberation when the time comes. It fights for liberty, equality, and fraternity, to use the immortal words of the great revolution.

This concludes in the main our discussion of social bias. Something will be added in the following chapter, and in future books I will develop this topic further on those points which have here remained unclear and blurred. This was inevitable because I lacked space for concrete evidence with which to support my general statements and suggestions. It is all the more necessary to do so because social bias is the important variable in education, as compared with the powerful constants that have occupied the foreground of my reflections.

The social function of education consists in the preservation of the biopsychic and socio-economic structure of society along with its cultural and intellectual attainments. Anything beyond this can be identified as a tendency to eternalize the existing distribution of power and concomitant psycho-social conditions. In that case, education is more than preservation or reproduction of what has been attained, it becomes conservation for the purpose of preventing anything new. We add one qualification: social bias enters education not simply to maintain the existing distribution of power, but to shift its balance in favor of the ruling and educating class. Seen from the latter's point of view, education is therefore conservative also in an ideational sense.

There can be no doubt that education fulfills this function. World reformers and moralists, educators and religious men may grieve about it, or they may grow jubilant over some ephemeral symptom as if it portended a permanent reversal, but children in any age grow up and become men typical of their time and place. It makes no difference whether they received an education, whether it was good or bad, or what method it adopted. The individual differences between them disappear and what remains is the great common herd of citizen sheep that yields the wool which returns the cost of breeding, care, and multiplying, plus a profit. They all look alike as sheep will, although the shepherd boy assures us that each has a face of its own. I doubt it and suspect that his love of them deceives him. What great difference can there be between one sheep's face and another? It's the wool, dear friends, that matters, and the wool, take it all in all, has grown well in this blessed year.

III

Ways, Means, and Possibilities
of Education

The heading of this chapter may have a calming effect upon the reader, and especially on the charming schoolmistress whose objections and agreement have repeatedly necessitated polemical qualifications on my part. Means of education—at last a term familiar from teachers' college years and an end to all those terrifying foreign words from Freud and ethnography. And even possibilities of education! This is heartening, for surely one cannot so entitle a chapter and come up with nothing at all. It is so encouraging, indeed, that the reader might now insist on having an answer to the question she raised near the end of Chapter I had she not long ago forgotten it and, like Ariadne in reverse, lost her thread in the labyrinth of the sociological chapter that followed. Instead of obliging her and developing its theme further, I leap way back—following my own invisible thread—and affirm that the answer has already been provided. The whole of pedagogy is a tool that serves the social bias of contemporary education. It is one of the means by which education fulfills its social function, not in the least meaningless and superfluous but supportive of the conservative function. Pedagogy provides the ideological justification for such educational actions as social bias dictates and does it so seductively as to create converts, blurring the distinction between socialist and capitalist education. The first could scarcely invent a better ideology than the second, and what happens in education is just a replay of the general power struggle of the bourgeoisie in which capitalist education uses socialist ideology to justify itself.

A sinister process is at work here. We have several times alluded to it, and it is time we looked into its devilish machinery. Who is it that rolls down the rock again as soon as Sisyphus has pushed it to the top of the mountain? It is the spite and malice of some great power that we must identify if Sisyphus is to be relieved of his suffering. The man has done useful work and gone about it intelligently, there is no reason why he should forever fail. Indeed, the Tartarus of the ancient Greeks looks like a pure educational affair, an odd assembly of pedagogues and other representatives of educational endeavor. Among them Tantalus is the most pitiful. Surrounded by refreshing water and delicious fruit, he need only stretch out his hand, it seems, to quench eternal thirst and hunger. But the cruel experience of centuries profits him nothing, fruit and water elude his grasp. What a symbol of the idealist theory of education! The realization of its ideal seems close at hand, requiring but a leap across some formal steps, yet it remains infinitely far away. Here too the magic trick of an offended deity seems to be at work. But whatever it is, Tantalus is justly punished for having cut up and sacrificed to the gods a sweet and merry boy—a horrible pedagogical deed frequently being committed. As to his colleagues, the Danaïds, these fifty young ladies may be appealing but their fate is uninteresting. They suffer from no secret spite, only from their own stupidity. Who can feel any sympathy for the attempt to fill a bottomless barrel with water? They should give it up instead of investigating the size and form of the leaky thimbles with which they draw the water. Sisyphus, however, does deserve our interest and sympathy even though his reputation should be badly tainted because he founded the Olympic Games, the Greek gymnasion, and, as a remote consequence though fortunately little known, the German *Gymnasium*. Yet his guilt, his boundless hubris, is not unpardonable. Why could not his rock for once remain at the top? It would not be the first time that presumption, long punished and derided, triumphed at last and received praise instead of being outlawed as a misdeed. Perhaps he does not even want our sympathy, perhaps he is glad to begin all over again, looks on his work as sport, and tips down the rock himself. If so, we will not betray him to the gods but will inquire only into the machinery which a spiteful fate employs at the behest of those offended personages.

How did it happen that Pestalozzi became the father of the public elementary school? What Circe transformed this kindhearted hotspur into a schoolmaster? Who substituted the monstrous German *Gymnasium* for Humboldt's pure idea? What sorcery turned Fichte's upright men into nationalist asses? The Socratic figures of recent centuries are allowed to live on, they are praised, and their ideas are realized in forms the very opposite of what they intended. I should think this is the pedagogical way to treat babies, to give them puppets with children's names instead of the real children they want. This is the way to treat pedagogues. They do not mind and do not want anything different. It hurts less this way. The aims and methods of education are the plaything, the favorite toy of educators.

Why should adults forbid them to play with them to their heart's content? Only they must be prevented from doing damage.

The question is not whether the ruling group succeeds in preventing any damage, but of how it is done so that the vanquished opposition thinks itself the victor. Instead of investigating the means of education, I inquire first into its ways and as far as I can see, I may be the first to do so. The pedagogical literature I have read and leafed through in the course of fifteen years does not bother about the dynamics of educational processes in society, the direction of educational progress, and the mutations the field undergoes. Yet these constitute the preliminaries for anyone who wants educational change and, through it, social change.

Most of what I am able to offer as an answer in the framework of this book is already contained, if scattered, in the preceding or can easily be derived from it. I will repeat it here, however, without any apologies. Two groups of forces, it seems, co-operate in instituting any specific type of education and education in general: these are psychological and social. We saw how education as a fact of nature originated in female and male forms in the biopsychic primal reaction of the mothers and the fathers of the horde to ontogenetic development. We saw how the psychic novelty, the sense of guilt which caused a transmutation of primeval society and economy, also transformed the original education and all socio-psychological reactions, though in primitive society it is impossible to tell which of its actions have a primary psychic origin and which are secondary or socially influenced. We saw what changes occurred in development itself: childhood became stretched out and complicated first by the insertion of the latency period and then by the prolongation of puberty. In the meantime the economy and its superstructure, including society, politics, and culture, brutally goes its own way and mankind finds itself the prisoner of the barbarism of a highly civilized capitalist epoch. It is uncertain about its path to freedom, but quite sure it was driven down this long road of sacrifice and torture without any profit or sense. It happened as a social consequence, the result of the economic system, the distribution of power, and class struggles. The power of economics is so great and pervasive that cultural history could be written explaining even the subtlest details of cultural life in economic terms. It looks as though education too is entirely determined by it, leaving no room for the effects of psychic reactions. Whether the newly born has a probability of 64 per cent or 9 per cent of bidding this world good-by as an infant is determined by where he is born, in "the proletarian hell of the Wedding district of Berlin" or in the Tiergarten section. The same fact decides whether he will experience the conflicts typical of the single or small-family child or those which befall the child of an eight- or twelve-member family. We know that the consequences of these conflicts ramify into the nuances of character formation. We know that the child, hovering in love and hate between its mother and father, following the path of its psychic development, which is laid out by inherited factors and directed and limited by its environment, becomes guilty of incestuous desires and parricidal thoughts, and that in the anxiety catastrophe of this innocent crime it acquires the internal authority of an unconscious sense of guilt. It becomes human through the superego, and all this is influenced by the fact that the family engages in procreative and economic activities, that the child is the family's possession, and that the child grows up within the family. How he grows up, with how much play and how much work, with what denials and what gratifications, what models and contents, must be ascribed to economics and its immediate consequences. At a certain age school begins, and what it offers in subject matter, human encounters, and morality is again the consequence of a definite industrial situation and its material requirements, of a given situation in the struggle for power between capitalism and socialism. The same holds true for the crucial decision by which a child is destined for a lengthy period of secondary and higher education or for the factory. Whether he reads this or that book depends not on its quality, but on whether he has ten pfennig or a hundred and fifty marks to spend for books. Which children's books reach the market depends not on their intrinsic merit, but on somebody willing to pay the printer; and he obviously expects to get his money back with interest and profit.

There is no end to these pompous banalities. Education costs money, and the money is in the hands of the bourgeoisie who would not think of investing it unprofitably. Least of all are they inclined to aid socialism in any way. Capital and the bourgeoisie are not interested in augmenting culture. What passes for culture consists exclusively in the satisfaction of their own cultural needs and in the securing of their material satisfactions through the ploy of ideology. Some individuals may be willing to expend money on culture without any thought of profit. There are limits to such generosity not only because even the greatest wealth is relatively circumscribed, but because the donor is victimized by the laws of capital. He loses to others who are more rational and moneyminded, and loses faster and substantially more than he puts at the disposal of culture. It would, of course, be nice to get capital away from the capitalists by ruses in order to provide proletarian children with a socialist education. But that is a Baron Münchhausen story. Modern man believes that to expropriate might almost be simpler, and one would not have to put off the benefits for a generation.

My most fundamental definition of education as the reaction of society to the fact of development takes all these circumstances into account. The economic structure of society provides the particular framework for this reaction. The organization of education is thoroughly determined and no part of it can be altered except through a preceding change of that structure. Education is inherently conservative and its organization especially so. Never has education prepared changes in the social structure. Always—without exception—it was the result of changes that had already taken place.

Would that mean there is no such thing as progress in education? No, none; at least not in the sense in which some anxious interlocutor may understand it. But has not illiteracy been practically eliminated in civilized, progressive countries and is this not to be credited to compulsory schooling? I do not regard the general ability to read and write as progress. Writing, like the railway or the radio, is a means of communication between people, though it has certain advantages over the other two in that it allows us to communicate also with the dead and the unborn. General literacy is similar to knowing how to use the railway or the airplane in that it is a culturally neutral affair. When someone takes a train to Rome, does he do it to elude the police in Vienna, to speculate on the Roman market, to admire the Sistine Chapel, or to compare the prices of wine? I remain unconvinced that writing and printing have been put to worthy use since compulsory schooling, or rather the invention of the rotary press made literacy widespread. It is not valid to object that railway travel need not be learned whereas reading must, and that it is the key to all cultural possibilities. Learning how to read has nearly become superfluous. It takes a halfway intelligent child scarcely a year of school, let alone seven years' compulsory attendance. In earlier times reading may have been a real art. But today, I wager, the whole trick is over and done with in a few weeks, or if educational methodology is employed, it takes a few months longer. At any rate, the whole matter is no longer a question of culture. It was different with the ancient Jews. For them reading meant intercourse with God, their supreme moral and cultural authority. Their primer was the Bible and the men at least had but one use for the acquired skill, the study of the Talmud which contained the entire cultural heritage. There were no other books. With us reading serves as a means of communication, perhaps already being made obsolete by radio and dictaphone and limited to special purposes. One may, it seems to me, entertain differing views of the value of reading for human progress. I do not regard illiterates a disgrace as long as they are "cultivated" in other respects.

But this is really not at issue. The fact is that compulsory schooling exists in all countries and has resulted in the spread of certain elementary knowledge which has promoted the progress not of knowledge itself but of capitalist development and the class struggle. For different reasons and historical circumstances, the opposing power groups involved both insisted on and obtained compulsory education after definite social advances had occurred, such as the Revolution of 1848 and, in a word, democracy. Socialism has every reason to rejoice over this gain, for it knows what to do with words and print. But it was not educational progress that made possible or prepared the advent of socialism. Rather, having reached a certain point in the growth of its power and altered the structure of society, socialism effected changes in educational organization of a kind that of course promoted a further growth of its power. Here the conservative function of education becomes very clear. It maintains the newly achieved structure, the new distribution of power, and in so doing augments it at times. Conservation becomes, so to speak, exponential and may from the socialist point of view be counted as progress. Socialism does indeed score advances which entail corresponding changes in education and which socialists value as progressive. But education itself is always backward. Its progress consists in its becoming a little less so.

We have now unexpectedly come upon a real and insurmountable limit of education. All education is conservative relative to the society that does the educating and it intensifies and increases the power of the educating group. The variable of education is, as I have said, only relative. Historically the organizational forms of education have undergone the most marked and rapid changes. In barely fifty years public youth care, for example, has grown and acquired extensive institutions. Juvenile law came into being within a few decades and educational tests developed within a few years. Compare education in ancient Persia as described by Xenophon with the monastic schools, universities, apprenticeships of the fourteenth century and with the life of youth in France at the time of the great Revolution, and you will discover if not absolute progress at least revolutionary changes. These are not, however, the realization of any ideas, aims, and projects of great or famous pedagogues. Nor are they the causes, but rather the results of cultural, social, intellectual, and perhaps psychic transformations that occurred in past centuries. They are not goal-oriented, they follow upon events as consequences. The feudal-militaristic social structure had its educational organization, whether it was in Mexico, Egypt, Japan, Persia, or ancient Germania. Modern capitalism too has its educational organization, no matter what the country, and it is adapted to each of its evolutionary phases, including the contemporary one. You don't like it? Neither do I, friend. But if you want to change it or some detail of it, you must first change the social structure or the correlative detail in it. If you want to introduce Fichte's educational organization, you must first create his economically self-sufficient state; or if you prefer a part of Plato's educational utopia, establish first the corresponding part of his Republic. There is no other way, everything else is idle fantasy.

This insight into the social limits of education negates any effort to effect marked changes in education before the social structure has been changed. It redirects one's energy to the central problem, which is social evolution or revolution, depending on whether one's desire for change is modest or bold. I shall presently express myself in favor of moderation without subscribing to that widespread reform theory which holds that a single innovative school can generate a thousand like it or that a model educational institution for middle-class youth can be copied for the proletariat. That theory is false. A few exceptional institutions may appear and continue for a time without prior change in the social structure. But their multiplication is something principally new and requires it absolutely.

This view is far from new. It follows directly from Marx's doctrine and the conclusions have been drawn in socialist writings. They can unfortunately not be found in the lit-

93

erature of education, and socialist educational writing, which is rather inferior, does not reflect on them with sufficient penetration. This is scarcely surprising for the consequences of the limitations of education imply a severe reduction in the power of education and of individual educators and their writings as well. The good citizen who is an idealist does not envy the money lender his personal power, nor does he begrudge the people's representatives of all stripes their political power because he scorns politics as ugly. Yet he will not tolerate any restrictions on spiritual power, such as he attributes to his ideas and writings. I would not deny that ideas and their propagandistic use may play a decisive role in the class struggle, and often have proved the final factor for victory on either side. Only their power—which in any case is far from absolute—does not reside within the ideas, just as their verbal expressions do not magically bring about rain, health, death, revolution, or moral perfection. The power of ideas is conferred on them by men whom the ideas have awakened, inspired, and emboldened. It makes sense to unite the proletariat of all countries through the ideas of the *Communist Manifesto* because this united class is able to effect real changes in the distribution of power by ordinary and nonspiritual means. But among children propaganda for morality does not make sense. Educators are too fearful and refined to concern themselves with the engine of social change and to serve this noisy and dangerous monster. They busy themselves with culture instead, and here again their fearfulness makes them turn to the children because they pose no threat to their persons or to their lust for omnipotence. "The weeding and sowing in children's souls" is an idyllic sort of farming. God continues the educators' work in his own way, he lets it rain and hail; and when harvest time comes round, the pedagogical sower is already gone to the dead or the blind. Thus his hope springs eternal, his professional pride remains unbroken.

Take, for example, this splendid passage of Pestalozzi's: "There is no salvation for the common people who are degraded morally, intellectually, and socially except through education, an education of man for humaneness. To lift the people up and to restore our dear degraded country, no salvation can be truly effective that does not begin with, and return to, a profound psychological study of the moral, intellectual, and artistic development of the human race." There are dozens of similar passages upon which Pestalozzi's fame rests. Yet given the social limitations of education they are nothing more than cowardly self-comfortings. It is simply impossible to create a culture of the people as long as the young land on the street or are handed over to the factory and forced labor at age twelve or fourteen. In such a situation the only meaningful demand is freedom from forced labor for everyone till his eighteenth year. Any other demand, no matter how noble its motive or immortal its words, merely serves to support the bias with which the capitalists administer education. It helps to preserve the existing state of culture which prevents the diffusion of cultural resources among "the people." It is the business of socialism and not of education to assert that meaningful demand to make it effective, and it is utopian until socialism has gained power.

This point is sufficiently important to be enlarged upon. The dissemination of culture is a highly personal affair, a concern of the human personality. We mean by this that the whole life and spirit of the individual should be permeated by the highest cultural values and possessions of the nation and mankind. Human personality develops

95

during adolescence when feelings and thoughts awaken which later form the nucleus of the cultural content and value of personality. If personality is to attain the highest standard possible for the average man, adolescence must have a certain complexity and its length must extend beyond the short period of physiological puberty well into the eighteenth or even twentieth year. With such freedom psychic development will not be inhibited, impoverished, and premature because of the individual's early need to work and his consequent economic independence. This freedom is indispensable if human development is to reach its full potential and the number of culturally mature personalities is to be maximized. It is not sufficient to guarantee the diffusion of culture. Once freed, youth must organize its life and give it content under the guidance of qualified persons.

Though presently displeased with this finite total result of education, the pedagogues will neither want to abandon their sphere of work nor surrender the flattering feeling of being active at the very center of things. But reason will at least compel them to recognize the social limits of education; and in retreating from a central to a peripheral position in human affairs, they may yet find comfort in the undeniable fact that despite the inevitable effects of educational institutions upon man, the educational process itself occurs within the individual; and individuals growing up in the same context differ considerably, for better or worse, and possess different degrees of culture.

In this last chapter where one is expected to be positive and conciliatory, I shall have to offend and disillusion some good and honest educators. I dislike doing so and would refrain from it altogether were I not convinced they won't be insulted, but will simply dismiss me as a cultural defeatist. According to their theory, education has to do with forming the individual personality and if all educators dedicated themselves to this task, society would eventually consist of high-minded, moral personalities. I cannot grow enthusiastic about the theory because it seems to me implausible that the educators' will can break down the barrier represented by the social limits of education. There exist in any period a number of individuals who by their psychic makeup, their attitude toward men and the world, their conception and fulfillment of duty, and their intellectual penetration appear to us as the desirable human average. We do not admire them as curious and incomparable pinnacles but view them as normal men and are astonished only by the many who do not measure up to them. It is my impression that such able, well made, and agreeable persons are less rare than in our peevishness we at times suppose. Are these then not living proof that satisfactory results can be achieved within the limitations of our society? Indeed they can, but we do not know the laws of their growth. Externally they live the same life, pass through similar families and schools, and undergo the same private and public experiences as others who deviate from this norm. Also as far as our primitive psychoanalytic methods allow us to judge, one group has the same psychic structure as the other. The admirable lot is a result of special influences we do not know and cannot even classify. They are a statistical fact of our education and their occurrence is as ordinary and regular as are suicides, burglars, the insane, and the murdered. Occasionally these figures change and then it may be possible to find the cause in a modification of the social structure, but usually the cause remains a mystery. The existence of those gratifying human specimens represents the pleasant side of social statistics, which for the most part is engaged in counting the less agreeable products, but it holds out little hope for the noble-minded young reader eager to turn the statistics upside down. Granted that one of the unknown preconditions for improvement is to find such a noble educator for the child, but here again the statistics average out. For as you, young friend, change your resigned wish to improve the lot of children so that a few more pleasant people may exist in the future, another young man just like you is simultaneously lost to the cause of education by being appointed professor of pedagogy.

Still, a chance of cheating the statistics may exist. The average good type we have been talking about is after all the normal man. We believe that every child could attain this norm unless prevented from doing so. Some of the obstructions we do not know, others can be identified. There are children who are reared under abnormal, inhuman conditions. Some never once have had enough to eat during the first ten years of their life. If these children were properly fed, their chance of growing and maturing normally would certainly increase and the statistics might be slightly altered. We may quote here the astonishment with which Pestalozzi reported the lesson of his first educational experiment: "It is a fact of experience that the most dejected children whom idleness and begging had weakened and deprived of health regained cheerfulness and strikingly good growth through steady if unaccustomed work. All that was necessary was to change their condition and to remove them from the causes and incitement of their passions. Experience has taught me that they rise quickly from their deep misery to the level of human feelings, to trust and friendship. Human kindness shown the lowliest of souls lifts them up, and the eyes of a wretched, abandoned child shine with deep-felt astonishment when a gentle hand reaches out in love toward him. In the depth of misery such a feeling can have important consequences for the morality and education of children."

The basic conditions of human growth include a measure of love. The child must feel loved and be allowed to love. It also needs to be denied, else unrestrained criminality or destructiveness may result. We know that optimal love is not sufficient to guarantee the desired result, but we also know that love is indispensable if the child is to approximate normal growth. At Neuhof, Pestalozzi entered the lives of those wretched children devoid of love and under his radiance they blossomed out—an experience which in the eighteenth century was unexpected and touching and in ours is moving and exhorting. You are right, young man, go where children are starved for love and give them what they need, which includes denial, and you will increase the chances for the development of a true humanity. But should you feel an urge to theorize, do not forget that you are necessarily a singular case; and unless militant socialism can protect you with its newly won position of power, your work will be forbidden should your example multiply. And, be good enough not to play the savior, you poor supernumerary; it doesn't suit you, and the children who love you might come to copy you, and then you would have negated your purpose.

Are there then no psychic powers, and is everything economically determined? No, these powers do exist and they determine everything, including the economy. This is one way of looking at things and it makes good scientific sense. Only it is of no help in pushing back the narrow limits set to educative work. Assuming some kind of psycho-social parallelism, scientific thought may abstract from and neglect one set of factors in favor of the other. But education that deals with reality will always be reminded of the as yet unknown relationship between the two: the social facts brutally break into the chain of conclusions drawn from the psychic facts.

It is, of course, true that the influence society exerts upon the growing generation through education is generally shaped by the favorable or unfavorable effect that individual adults have on individual children. It is here that possibilities open for education. Unhappily, the adults themselves are products of that opaque cluster of influences we call education and therefore unfit to be the agents of a different education that seeks to accomplish revolutionary transformations in the human soul. This is the circularity to which education is condemned and within which pedagogy vainly gropes for the new educators of the new men. For education does not consist merely of what professional educators do or think they do but of what countless individuals and society as a whole do. In the vault of the central bank pure gold is stored in heavy ingots, but what we see and daily handle and live on are the torn, dirty small bills whose value derives from that central treasure. Occasionally a clean crisp bill comes our way and we may save it for a few days. Similarly, the image of some individual, who in one way or the other taught us, may be retained, perhaps even forever, because he affected us so deeply. Each love leaves a permanent residue within us, becomes part of our character and personality. This includes our love for official educators, but before that came the more crucial love for parents and people who were part of our earliest environment. Love does not necessarily ask for value and moral perfection and its residue in us is not the equal of the loved person's value. Hence the chances look dim for our noble young man who wants to change the world through education.

It will be said that I am spreading disillusionment. I do not agree, for I do not understand why educational work should be charged with such extravagant hopes. Does a good cobbler expect any more from his work than to make money and, if he is a craftsman, to produce decent shoes? Is he going to be disillusioned if I tell him that his work will no more bring God to earth than it will realize morality, culture, and socialism? Does a physician need more than an income and the satisfaction of curing the sick? Why should culture and humanity be any concern of the educator? Is it not sufficient for him to foster those who need it, to play with children, which they like, to instruct them, which they like less but which is also good for them. Why the great extra wish of helping shape the future in accordance with a veritable orgy of ultimate ideals? And then to be disillusioned when this ideal is crossed off the list?

These are not rhetorical questions. They are answerable, and the answer is on two levels. The mass of ordinary teachers will trade whatever stormy higher ambitions they may have for a commensurate increase in salary. Let them make a decent living by instruction and their work will seem to them self-sufficient and rational without hitching it to the starry heaven of ideals. Others who are less simply built will remain discontented for reasons that lie in the very nature of education. Education as a pair-group activity cannot satisfy the adult and hence his search for compensation in those ideals.

The educator's dissatisfaction has a number of reasons, some of which have already been referred to. They all ultimately derive from the fact that the true educator, whose supposed disillusionment alone is at issue, has chosen his profession from a love of children, and that this love remains unfulfilled. It is indeed a paradoxical love. What business has an adult anyway to love children that are not his own? I do not mean merely that he occasionally enjoys their company and is diverted by their gaiety. I mean the kind of love that becomes his principal occupation so that he seeks to live and care for the young and is unable to be without their company. This proves that a powerful love urge dwells in his unconscious, though consciously he may feel little of its press and experience neither longing nor gratification. Adults as a rule do not love children, apart from their own, whom they must love because they may not hate them. Children disturb, make noise and dirt, talk nonsense, and are a nuisance in many ways. One avoids them if possible; if not, annoyance, hostility, and dislike soon come to be expressed. The kind uncle whose whim it is to love children is laughed at and excused; he does not know what they are really like, in an unloving environment. The educator is the kind uncle who has elevated the whim to his profession. He simply loves children and chose the profession because it permits him continuous contact with the objects of his love.

Love is a beautiful word. It is strange that language anticipated Freud's discoveries by employing the same word to designate a strong fondness for any object, be it landscapes, women's legs, alcohol, science, God, pink ribbons, or children. Language regards desire itself the important thing, being always the same regardless of its object and having a certain quality difficult to define but easy to poetize. Freud calls it libido or eros. Our prudish time,* how-

* Psychoanalysts are in the habit of talking about this hypocritical prudery because their science suffers much from it. I dwell on it because I expect my readers to include parents and educators, and every-

ever, exempts certain objects as impure and impermissable. Money, anthroposophy, war, and our splendid social order are not among these, but love for the other sex is—the love which moves us most and grants the highest bliss, which perpetuates our "earthly existence," and links us with the rest of the organic world. To preserve the purity of the other objects, abysmal differences are alleged to exist between sexual love and all other types. This is too preposterous for language, which calls all love by the same term. I may choose to submit to our arbitrary valuation, respect it if I want to live in peace, but I cannot surrender my intellectual integrity to it. This has become impossible since Sigmund Freud in fearless defiance of prudery recognized sexual love as the original and essential and all others as derivative and deflected from their true goal. This view implies no value judgment. Any preacher is free to condemn genital love as impure while declaring the *disciplina gynopygica* as sacred. All the same, this derivative love, deflected from its original goal precisely by such value judgment, remains the original love. And in the black soul of that preacher the same old love for its original object lives on in the still blacker dungeon of the repressed unconscious, driving him on to loud sermons and light temptations to which I hope he will sometimes submit.

It is such goal-deflected love that drives the educator to "his" children. To say this is not to devalue his work but to make intelligible the educator's contradictions. Deflected love is more complicated than direct love for in addition to

one is still prudish in these matters today. Though the number of shameless people has grown greatly in the last two decades, it should not be forgotten that deliberate shamelessness, like prudery, springs from the same fatal psychic situation. One attitude can suddenly change into the other. Neither extreme provides the atmosphere in which the science of education or the science of psychology can thrive.

creating situations of deep satisfaction, it provides others of intense dissatisfaction. Freud used the term sublimation for the libido that is deflected from its sexual goal to another, culturally highly valued one. The educator's love for children is genuine but sublimated. A child is not a suitable object for adult sexual love and if it becomes such, we consider it a perversion or crime. This condemnation itself renders the child wholly inappropriate as an object of direct satisfaction. If an educator ever felt such inclination, he would resolutely repudiate it, banish it from his consciousness, and successfully prevent its issue into action. Perhaps there is some tenderness in his love of children, but even that is not required because he loves the child "in general" and devotes himself to its development and future. The measure of sublimated, sublime love a person has at his disposal is a basic character trait usually acquired in early youth. On it an individual's social value really depends because such love is truly selfless; it is self-fulfilling and for its ministrations requires no more of its object than acceptance. There is still the question as to what objects are chosen, whether stamps or children, and whether the ministrations consist of flogging or kindness. The modern educator chooses a significant love object and his services are kind, thereby making him an admirable, even enviable person. The only trouble is that among us moderns genuine sublime love is in short supply. There is not enough to teach a single child the elements of reading or to listen to a young man's conflicts.

This deficit is balanced by a libido which, seemingly sublime, is in truth undeflected from, but frustrated in, its original satisfactions. Of such frustrated love the educator has more than his share. Reared in a society built on hatred whose trade marks are competition, exploitation, war, private property, and profit, his Oedipal wishes since childhood have never been cultivated or satisfied. They are stunted, repressed, or brutalized. When they are allowed satisfaction, it is lame and feeble, guilt ridden, neurotically hasty, or burdened with conflicts which it is preferable to escape by renouncing the pleasure. Our good educators, however, are not even allowed to indulge themselves. So they repress their desire for a woman, a man, or a child, for love and self-confidence, and transfer it to other people's children, who could not satisfy it if they wished. Thus the apparently sublime love of the educator carries within it the germ of deepest dissatisfaction because it is sublime not by choice but out of need, and therefore will just barely do. It is incapable of withstanding the least stress.

We need to penetrate still farther into the structure of the psyche and the resistance raised against Freud's teaching to reach the second level of our answer. His principal discovery, we recall, was that every child develops a strong affection for the parent of the opposite sex and violent hostility to the rival, the parent of its own sex. The boy loves his mother and wants to assume the father's place and dominion, reacting to the latter's resistance with impulses of murder, vengeance, dislike, and aggression. He finds himself in the situation attributed by legend to Oedipus who, unknowingly but guilty all the same, slew his father and slept with his mother. Similarly the child grows into the Oedipal situation innocently and unconsciously, and then is pronounced guilty by his own ego. The Oedipus situation is a necessary phase of human development which takes three to five years to get into and another few to outgrow. It cannot be skipped even if the child—like the orphan cited as the living refutation of psychoanalysis—is not reared by his natural parents. In this case the child will find suitable substitute figures. Intricate family relations complicate the Oedipus situation, that is all—though even that is not certain. We do not yet fully understand the conditions under which its manifold variations are produced or avoided. At any rate, no child can grow up in a family or pair group without acquiring the Oedipus complex. Its resolution is the decisive way-station in the child's psychic development. As the infantile phase comes to an end, a large number of infantile desires, experiences, and urges is split off from the ego abd driven into the unconscious. The ego is purged of all traces, memories, and experiences of the original crimes of incest and parricide. Guilt, conscience, and a whole superstructure of ideals, aims, and laws secure it against any breakthrough of what has been repressed. Still, what has been repressed is by no means eliminated. Everything repressed remains secretly alive and acts lastingly and resolutely upon the ego's thought, deeds, and especially love life. But what is repressed is also deformed; the ego fails to recognize it, or even to notice it because it is unconscious. The repressed elements pursue a fanatically and cleverly retained goal: to restore the infantile situation with all its desires, fulfillments, and destinies. Where, whom, and what we love—the same repressed elements always act within us, and they love only as they once loved, but with those deformities, corrections, and compromises that the ego can and must enforce lest it come face to face with the one great original crime.

If any relationship between child and educator exists at all, it will on both sides develop into the Oedipal type. The child will love or hate the educator as it did the father or mother, or it will have a love-hate relationship with him. The child confronts the educator with the same old wishes —impetuously, obstinately, or slyly if need be—and is driven to a repetition of their fate. What else can the educator do but accept the role thrust upon him whether or not he loves the child. He continues the parents' work albeit with other means, or he repeats it in a way that is new to the child: he works toward the destruction of the Oedipus complex even though the child's sexual love for him is not incest and its aggression not parricide. All the same, the educator we have in mind loves the child and assumes his role willingly, with enthusiasm and devotion, under the influence of his own Oedipus complex. The child before him is he himself as a child who experienced the same desires, conflicts, and fate. The actual differences between them matter little, being only differences in their egos, not in their urges and desires. What he does, what he grants and prohibits, is what his parents did to him. In the pedagogical pair group he appears in the double role of child and educator; and as if this were not complicated enough, he is in his educative role not himself, but divided into a thinking, acting ego and an ego-alien power, to wit, his own repressed urges that both inhibit and drive him on. Thus he faces two children: the one before him to be educated and the other repressed within him. He really has no choice but to treat the former the same way in which he experienced the latter, for what's good for the goose is good for the gander. He repeats the destruction of his own Oedipus complex with the other child as with himself. This is true even if he appears to do the opposite of what his parents did to him.

Obviously I perceive this pedagogical situation in highly complicated terms, and in this affective vortex the reader's hope of finding rational, purposive action guided by principles and the results of empirical investigation must be fading. He may at least see profound possibilities for the educator's satisfaction if the three partners—the child before him, the one in him, and his own ego—come together in harmony in this great repetition. Profound dissatisfaction, however, is equally likely and in the long run it is practically inevitable. For both children want to re-experience the Oedipus situation whereas the ego wants to repeat its destruction. The ego responds with guilt feelings or its numerous equivalents, which do not have to be enumerated to those informed about psychoanalysis, and which to the uninformed cannot be explained in a subsidiary clause. All the responses produce unpleasure,[12] inhibition, and aversion. The repressed child within the teacher knows how to avenge itself when the love situation rejected by the ego is about to reappear and gratification is denied. The educator will therefore react to the child before him with annoyance, severity, inconsistency, and persecution, all directed really at himself but vented upon the other. He thereby loses the love which, within permitted bounds, he sought to win. In this situation he will justify himself with the argument of idealist pedagogy. In losing the love of his young charge, he seeks to earn the thanks of mankind for promoting its happiness. At the same time, he succeeds in silencing the guilt created by the harmony of love between the two children. Though wicked in itself, this union becomes permissible by being sanctified as the means of transforming and saving mankind.

At this juncture some minor and major questions, which I have only alluded to or suppressed entirely, might be pursued and answered. I shall have to leave them to the reader to puzzle out because this book is about the limits of education and has at this late stage arrived at only one of them.

[12] In psychanalytic literature unpleasure is the standard translation for *Unlust*, meaning a state of instinctual, disagreeable tension.—*Tr.*

This is the limit defined by the psychic realities within the educator himself. A second one, encountered long ago but now explicitly recognized as such, is found in the psychic constants that place restrictions on all grand pedagogical projects. The third limit, to which we now proceed more quickly and which readers have been expecting all along, lies in the educability of the child. Of the three, the last is most familiar and widely recognized. Every pedagogical Baedeker recommends that one obtain a clear idea of the psychological potential as well as the resistance which child nature offers to educational effort. For this reason I left this topic to the end and explored first the more winding and rewarding paths of which the pedagogical guides know nothing.

Pedagogues have occasionally expressed themselves quite pessimistically about the educability of the child, so much so that they should really have declared the whole enterprise futile. My own view tends in that direction, but is not quite that bleak. Of course, under the influence of Darwinism, the doctrine of heredity, and determinist psychology it was easy enough to imagine that the course of human life was predetermined at the moment of conception. What followed seemed no more than a wound-up puppet show, and only those children who did not know of the mechanism and understand it could think that the puppets moved freely. Actually the determinist is no better off than those children, but worse: since he cannot predict how the puppets will move, he must treat them as if they were free agents though he knows they are not. If he happens to be an educator, he will say that the child will behave as its inner springs dictate regardless of his educational efforts. However, the shock of Darwinism and the theory of inheritance has passed, and we know that men are by no means like puppets. True, man's fate is predetermined, yet it requires a certain milieu, certain experiences, and external influences to be actualized. A man's life consists of recapitulation, but not of the life of the father or original ancestor. Something of our own is added because we live under certain conditions in a certain time and place. Individual life is a singular unique nuance introduced into general recapitulation by the fact of its concrete localization. The individual traits of life are a system of accidents that force a compromise on general recapitulation. My life is only one interpretation of the latter, but given the combination of all relevant circumstances, it is the only possible one.

An individual is an entity of many layers. They reach all the way from the uniformities he shares with billions of other organisms up to the ego with its own unique face and destiny. But it is this uppermost and thinnest layer that matters most to the individual because it alone belongs to him exclusively. The chance events that produced it are perceived by him as personal experiences, they are his fate. He resists any attempt to view them as meaningless accidents, but prefers to read in them the guidance of a benevolent divinity or, like Wilhelm Meister,[13] of a secret conclave of men. He feels like thanking educators for his individuality, and indeed this individual layer is significant for education in the narrower sense of the term. To deny that significant effects can be achieved on this level would be wrong and stupid, for education is part of the system of accidents whose individuation we call life. Susceptibility to outside influence is limited and variable but all the same

[13] A reference to Goethe's pedagogical novel *Wilhelm Meisters Lehrjahre* (Part I, 1795) and *Wilhelm Meisters Wanderjahre* (Part II, 1828).—*Tr.*

considerable. We may venture the slightly optimistic statement that while the child is by no means as malleable as wax, it is far more plastic than metal. The precise degree and limits of his malleability remain an important problem, to the solution of which the science of education has so far contributed little.

From this lack of knowledge, educational theory as now constituted cannot draw much comfort. Even if human malleability were unlimited, individual prognoses would remain doubtful. It profits educational theory little to know —even if it were true—that every educational action has some influence on the child that will show up in his future character and adult behavior. The knowledge it needs is what specific result will flow from a specific action, and even the most progressive psychology conceivable cannot furnish predictions of this order. The reason lies in the very nature of the psychic life. When two chemical elements are combined under identical controlled conditions, the result is always predictable. The hydrogen and oxygen combined by the chemist to obtain water have no history, their previous experiences and spatial location are irrelevant to their chemical interaction. Two children subjected to identical educational treatment may show identical reactions, but this is not certain because each has its own history that affects every psychic reaction. It is impossible to know exactly how a child will behave in a planned educational situation, what its effect and the duration of the effect will be. Not even a knowledge of the individual's history can appreciably increase the predictability. In so far as individuals share a common history, their actions will be similar. But this resemblance, which is indeed striking, derives from the nonindividual layers of the human psyche. The business of pedagogy is with the individual layers.

Moved by a more or less dim recognition of these facts, some educators have decided to set their own as well as mankind's hopes on Freud. But this is due to a misunderstanding, if not a want of intelligence. Only since Freud have we begun to understand the psychic life and childhood, and so far psychoanalysis is the only method of inquiring into a person's psychic history. In a sense, it is an historical method; it tells us what influence accidents had upon the individual's formation and how this influence may be distinguished from the general recapitulative tendency. Psychoanalysis has provided general insights and taught us to identify general behavioral patterns of the human psyche, but applied to the individual subject, it remains historical. Though it can ascertain and illumine past reactions, it cannot predict future reactions with certainty although it may at least project alternative probabilities. For example, of a particular child about to be subjected to a certain educational treatment, it may predict either repression or sublimation as the likely reaction and deduce further probable consequences from these alternatives. For the present even this is too much of a gamble. In short, we conclude that psychoanalysis is of no help to educational theory because the latter needs individual prognosis for the individual child John Smith. And individual pedagogy is served no better by the optimistic view of the malleability of the child. Every educational action remains, therefore, a promissory note that falls due in twenty years. In the meantime no one will endorse it because the debtor's credit is unascertainable—it doesn't matter whether the child or his teacher is to be regarded as the debtor in this dubious affair.

Still, the child's malleability does warrant a good deal of optimism. While individual prognoses remain unreliable, a collective prognosis is feasible based on the common historical lot of men and the similarity of their psychic behavior. Psychoanalytic knowledge of human history in both its general and individual dimension, combined with the experience educational science provides, enables us to make group prognoses to the effect that a majority of the children will react in a certain way to a proposed treatment. No conceivable remedial action can guarantee to rehabilitate a neglected, abandoned child, but some means promise at least a measure of probable success. If the subject of concern is no longer the individual John Smith but an entire age group of children, the value of the collective prognosis changes appreciably: it then provides clear information, on the basis of which the merit and desirability of a certain program can be determined. In a socialist society a program guaranteeing success with, say, 80 per cent of the children will be adopted. Whose children are included in the successful percentage and whose will be left out is of no interest here. The precise opposite holds true for contemporary educational theory that aims to score a certain success with John Smith while remaining indifferent to the fate of millions.

A comparison with military strategy suggests itself here, which—alas—employs the methods of socialist mass-societies to kill men, while the more peaceful and sympathetic realm of education has adopted the murderous means of capitalism. An army commander calculates the losses he must expect from an offensive. If he can absorb them, he will risk the offensive and be content if his estimate does not prove too low. Whether John Smith will be among the dead or the living—to his relatives and friends justly the most important fact about the entire war—does not concern the commander at all. Now education, no matter what social order it serves, will always care about the individual's lot. A society concerned for the education of all its children —and not just of John Smith—can and must develop a rational plan for the educational system as a whole and for the assignment of priorities within it. By utilizing our insights into the psychology of the child and its development, and our knowledge of human constants and the social approaches to educational problems, we should manage to stay fairly free of ideological justifications for unconscious desires and even of the hidden bias of the ruling minority.

The possibilities for education lie here, within the three boundaries previously defined. I hope the reader will not suspect me of wishing to transplant education and its theory to a walled-in, sheltered place while leaving it otherwise unchanged. He has not forgotten, I hope, that the educability of the child cannot be fully exploited by individual educators alone, and that the collective prognosis is directed not at this narrower individual dimension but at the whole educational enterprise understood as the reaction of society to all the facts of human development. If education is to be turned to some use and to be deliberately shaped by the will and purposes of a group, it must be rescued from the exclusive domination of the individualist perspective. The future individual adult is not predictable, an individual educator's actions aiming to produce him are never decisive. The Oedipus complex at the base of all personal educational relationships prevents their being controlled by rational purposes. A collectively oriented aim and prognosis, taking account of the totality of relevant educational factors, are realizable only in a socialist society; in a society steeped in the ideology of the ruling capitalist group, they are impossible.

This assertion is meant as a rational conclusion, not a

confession. If this book has been more forthright, the author's personal and affective position more visible, than becomes a scientific treatise, it is neither a work of art where imagination and feeling are allowed free play nor a piece of political propaganda arguing solely in support of the party point of view. The book is the outcome of scientific insights, constructions, and attitudes. I do not wish to agitate for socialism by presenting it as the flawless, desirable future promising total salvation. How far it will in time satisfy men and bring peace to humankind is still very much in doubt. My only purpose is to state that socialism and education under it are necessarily related, and that socialism constitutes that political order in which pedagogy *can* become a science. Then pedagogy would no longer be obliged to present its insights in a manner that lends itself to the justification of capitalist interests. Nor will it need to adjust its inquiries to the interests of the individual possessive parent. As long as the science of education is required to answer questions relating essentially to the pair group—and these alone benefit the bourgeois-capitalist order—it cannot find a solid foundation. (All this is meant to state facts, not yet to judge them.)

Capitalism cannot tolerate a science of education. No academic chairs, institutes, or publishing houses will be endowed in its name, and it will not be empowered to destroy the superstition that pretends to be the pedagogy that is necessitated by the psychic constants. On the contrary, all incipient attempts at enlightenment will be interfered with as soon as they have reached a degree of visibility, because the whole society is erected upon the Oedipus situation of the child and its characteristic form of destruction. Hence, educational practice and its ideology, the theory of education, are devoted to the preservation of that basis. An independent educational science would show that actual educational practice reflects social causes and psychic preconditions, but that its pedagogical justification is sheer superstition. Such a science can be developed despite the opposition of the ruling group if socialism is sufficiently powerful to foster it, and I believe it has reached that stage. The idea of an absolutely free science is a myth that merely serves to conceal its dependence. In socialist society, too, the individual scholar, the whole enterprise of science, its type of inquiry, and much of its methods will encounter material and intellectual limitations. Present dependencies will be exchanged for others, science will certainly not be free. To us at least those future dependencies seem more tolerable and productive than those which now prevail; how the actual participants will judge them remains an open question. We would do well to bear this in mind and speak of a socialist science of education, which though not *the* science, is nevertheless a desirable science. Socialism, it seems to me, already has the power to promote it and by so doing would strengthen its own position.

But the socialists themselves are unaware of this possibility. They remain backward in their educational views, far below the level they have reached in other social questions, and they fail to take advantage of the power they already have. The working masses and even the farsighted leaders among them have not grasped the idea of a collective education and of planned educational action. They are imprisoned in the bourgeois educational conception whose structure is psychically and socially individualist and whose process consists in repeating and then destroying the Oedipus situation, always within the confines and according to the model of the family or pair group. By its own backwardness, present day socialism thus imposes still another limit upon the possibilities of education. Yet this limit is surmountable. Why should socialism, having learned that the real issue is not the redistribution of income but the creation of a new social structure, not also learn that the issue in education is not to make secondary and higher education available to the proletarian child but to develop a new educational system? This insight will dawn on men as soon as they achieve power—we have seen it happen in Soviet Russia. But it can begin to be learned even now, and one hopes this will be done, though it is not necessary to assert that the attainment of a higher level in matters of socialist education is of surpassing importance to the development of socialism itself.

The question of the educability of the child and how to promote it is not really pivotal here. I have already indicated my qualified optimism in this regard. We have no reason to assume that the individual's recapitulation of mankind's history extends as far as the superstructure of the super-ego and the destruction of the Oedipus complex. Upward from the age of four or six, the child's development is fully within the sphere of educability. Drives, general mechanisms, and behavioral patterns certainly exist and operate independently of environmental influence, whereas the content of psychic life, the fate of the drives, the structure of the ego and super-ego are in part shaped by it. Environmental changes produce changes in individuals that are collectively predictable. Such changes are enforced by means of unpleasure and denial, which, whether deliberately decreed by the educator or a part of the environment, come into opposition to the accustomed behavior, inherited or acquired. They necessitate suppression, repression, sublimation, and identification. Unpleasure, anxiety, and guilt are the agents through which educability is actualized and made concrete. These are not without danger because they may repel a child, even to the extreme of idiotic alienation, from the denying, anxiety- and guilt-producing world. Compensation in the form of substitute pleasures must therefore be provided. But as these are always of questionable value, the environment will have to be shaped so as to require relatively few renunciations. It will have to be adapted to the strengths of children, their maturity, vitality, and need for pleasure if they are to grow up in harmony with it. Else, turning away from it in neurosis and crime, or turning upon it with unbridled hostility, they may atrophy or regress to an animal-like existence.

Once again we have unmistakably reached the social limitation. Yet when we ask how renunciation can at all be made acceptable, we come upon an odd and, at first, encouraging fact. It is wonderfully easy to influence children and even adolescents and to induce in them quite remarkable changes. Even badly neglected, criminal children change fundamentally if they are removed from their milieu and placed in a well-ordered child community. A patient demonstration of love will awaken their own love, and by consistently denying them the primitive love goals that begin to stir in them, they can be forced to identify with the teacher, their fellows, and the community. Unconsciously and without reflection, Pestalozzi accomplished this at Neuhof and Stanz. Freud has since taught us how to understand such transformation in children, and this should guard us from the danger to which Pestalozzi succumbed. He felt the power of love, observed its effects, and generally recognized it as an essential ingredient of education. Unhappily, misguided by his collaborators Niederer and Schmidt, he shifted the emphasis of his work and relied increasingly on instructional method, ascribing both the fault and the merit of his system to it alone. This was equivalent to theoretically depreciating, if not actually repressing, the libidinal drives of educator and children. It was the price he paid for the assent of his time, all the way from the tsar of Russia to the dry pastor of a Swiss village. As an old man and still alert, he rued his error though even then he concealed the essential thing behind accidentals. We may learn from him, and psychoanalysis can guide us better than he.

What is true of wayward children applies no less to children in the family who become sick, disagreeable, unmanageable, and give cause for anxiety. How many of them blossom out as soon as they have escaped the ban of the Oedipus situation! Renunciation then becomes easier for them; and because of such willingness and the greater educability attained in an appropriate setting, education has one great possibility. It can be realized through the organization of child life in special institutions that will bring growth, flowering, and harmony to an overwhelming majority of children. The establishment of such institutions depends upon the prevailing social conditions. Possibly their attraction is diminished by our ignorance of whether those reared in them will turn out to be any different from other adults. Their improvement remains more than doubtful. Perhaps, however, the readiness for renunciation and education of which we spoke suggests that this characteristic was acquired by earlier generations, and that we therefore were born better equipped morally than we suppose. In that case the outlook is more promising. Educability may continue rather than terminate with adulthood if youth enters a society that has use for the pleasant, normal type of man instead of transforming or destroying him. In that ideal society it may no longer matter at all how children are brought up, for identification in any case will turn them into just men. There is no end to ambivalence and doubt. A scientist is not ashamed of them—he exaggerates them in order, he hopes, to overcome them in the future.